PRAISE FOR *PUBLISH YOUR PURPOSE*

"It's a miracle I learned to read, let alone write a book. Speaking of reading, there is no book if there is no reader. I stumbled through the writing process, unaware of its complexity. I stumbled again when it came time to shepherd my book to an actual shelf. There is a sea of confusing and questionable industry resources. *Publish Your Purpose* is the outlier—in the best way. The PYP team is a family consisting of thought partners, champions, and good citizens. Plus it's a good business. Their model makes a difference, so the writers they represent can do the same. Together, the voices for justice are stronger. Thank you PYP, Jenn, and the entire team."

—**Lisa Wise,** Founder & Chief Strategist of Flock D.C., Speaker, Bestselling Author of *Self-Elected: How to Put Justice Over Profit and Soar in Business*

"Putting one's purpose into words and sharing them with an audience can be an overwhelming endeavor, but Jenn's approach makes it possible. The wisdom she shares within these pages is changing the world, one person's story at a time."

—**Erin Weed,** TEDx Speaker on Authentic Communication, Creator of The Dig® and of Head-Heart-Core®

"*Publish Your Purpose* completely changed my perspective on becoming an author. This book is an incredibly insightful and comprehensive guide for anyone looking to write and publish their own book. Part 1 of the book, "Mindset," sets the tone for the rest of the journey by focusing on personal and professional goals, getting into the right mindset, and holding yourself accountable. This part really helped me understand the importance of purpose and vision when writing a book."

—**Nell Derick Debevoise,** Chief Wrangler, Inspiring Cowgirl PBC, Bestselling Author of *Going First: Finding the Courage to Lead Purposefully and Inspire Action*

"*Publish Your Purpose* is an essential read for any aspiring author. Jenn's comprehensive guide covers everything from picking the best publishing path for you to managing your publishing costs and timeline. But what really sets this book apart is Jenn's insight into the dangers of scams and censorship and her practical advice for avoiding them. If you're serious about publishing your work, this book is a must-have resource."

—**Tina Dietz,** CEO of Twin Flames Studios, Award-Winning and Internationally Acclaimed Audiobook and Podcast Producer

"Mindset is one key to success, and *Publish Your Purpose* is a fantastic guide for anyone who wants to cultivate a winning mindset. Jenn provides practical and actionable advice on how to identify your purpose, vision, and impact, and how to set personal, professional, and business goals. What I loved most about this book is that it not only teaches you how to get into the right mindset but also provides strategies for staying accountable and how to promote your book along the way. Jenn's writing style is engaging and easy to follow, and I found myself nodding along and taking notes throughout the book. I highly recommend this book to anyone who wants to take their mindset to the next level and achieve their goal of writing and publishing a book."

—**Victoria (Vikki) Brown,** Founder of V.A. Brown Consulting

"If you have a book inside you that wants to come out but don't know how to go about it or struggle to get started or finish it, this book is written just for you. I felt compelled to write my book. I started to write it, then started again, and again, and again. I was clear on why I was writing it, but I was not clear about who I was writing it for. Once I was clear on that, it just flowed. This book will help you get clear on your purpose, your vision, and who you are writing for. Jenn has suggestions for what to do at each step of the process to keep you on track and accountable to yourself. She makes the publishing process and publisher options easy to understand. It is important to choose a publisher based on the relationship you want to have with one. A supportive and collaborative publisher is essential to a good book."

—**Gavin Watson,** Board Chair of Conscious Capitalism Connecticut, Author of *Altruistic Business*

"*Publish Your Purpose* is a must-read for anyone considering publishing a book. Jenn covers all the important topics, from determining your unique publishing needs and desires to avoiding scams and censorship. Her insights on picking the best publishing path for you and what questions to ask publishers are invaluable. She also provides practical advice on managing your publishing costs and timeline, as well as planning a successful book launch and beyond. I highly recommend this book to anyone looking to make their publishing dreams a reality."

—**Jennifer Brown,** DEI Thought Leader, Keynote Speaker, Bestselling Author of *How to Be an Inclusive Leader, Beyond Diversity,* and *Inclusion*

"I've had the benefit of participating in Publish Your Purpose's writing program. This book is the next best thing to having the Publish Your Purpose team connecting with you daily. This book is a comprehensive guide to the writing and publishing journey and lets each author define their own path. *Publish Your Purpose* balances practical application with the emotional process of putting one's all into words."

—**Erna Alfred Liousas,** CCXP, Founder & CEO of U*REALIZED

"As someone who has been navigating the world of book publishing for years, I can confidently say that *Publish Your Purpose* is an indispensable resource for authors of all levels. Jenn provides valuable insights into everything from identifying your publishing needs and desires to avoiding the challenges the industry offers. Her guidance around picking the best publishing path for you is particularly helpful, as she breaks down the pros and cons of each option and provides a list of questions to ask potential publishers. Whether you're a first-time author or a seasoned pro, *Publish Your Purpose* is an essential read for anyone looking to publish their book."

—**Stephanie Feger,** Book Marketing Strategist and Founder of the emPower PR Group, Author of *Make Your Author emPact: Sell More Books, Increase Your Reach & Achieve Your Why*

PUBLISH YOUR PURPOSE

PUBLISH YOUR PURPOSE

A Step-By-Step Guide
To Write, Publish, and
Grow Your Big Idea

JENN T. GRACE

Copyright © 2023 Jenn T. Grace. All rights reserved.

No part of this publication shall be reproduced, transmitted, or sold in whole or in part in any form without prior written consent of the author, except as provided by the United States of America copyright law. Any unauthorized usage of the text without express written permission of the publisher is a violation of the author's copyright and is illegal and punishable by law. All trademarks and registered trademarks appearing in this guide are the property of their respective owners.

For permission requests, write to the publisher, addressed "Attention: Permissions Coordinator," at the address below.

Publish Your Purpose
141 Weston Street, #155
Hartford, CT, 06141

The opinions expressed by the author are not necessarily those held by Publish Your Purpose.

Ordering information: Quantity sales and special discounts are available on quantity purchases by corporations, associations, and others. For details, contact the publisher at hello@publishyourpurpose.com.

Edited by: Malka Wickramatilake and Nancy Graham-Tillman
Cover design by: Rebecca Pollock
Typeset by: Nelly Murariu

Printed in the United States of America.

ISBN: 979-8-88797-091-2 (paperback)
ISBN: 979-8-88797-067-7 (ebook)

Library of Congress Control Number: 9798887970653

First edition, October 2023.
1.3

The information contained within this book is strictly for informational purposes. The material may include information, products, or services by third parties. As such, the Author and Publisher do not assume responsibility or liability for any third-party material or opinions. The publisher is not responsible for websites (or their content) that are not owned by the publisher. Readers are advised to do their own due diligence when it comes to making decisions.

Publish Your Purpose is a hybrid publisher of non-fiction books. Our mission is to elevate the voices often excluded from traditional publishing. We intentionally seek out authors and storytellers with diverse backgrounds, life experiences, and unique perspectives to publish books that will make an impact in the world. Do you have a book idea you would like us to consider publishing? Please visit PublishYourPurpose.com for more information.

DEDICATION

To Leena, Samson, and Peaches.

Your dedication to lying across the keyboard while I typed was unmatched. Without your steadfast commitment, this book would have been completed much sooner.

And to Cameron, for being the best son and cat daddy we could ask for.

CONTENTS

Preface   xv
Introduction   xxiii

PART 1: MINDSET   1

1   Your Purpose, Vision, and Impact, Oh My!   3
2   Your Goals: Personal, Professional, and Business   21
3   Getting into the Right Mindset   35
4   Accountability and Support Systems   47

PART 2: WRITING   63

5   Your Target Reader   65
6   How Long Should Your Book Be?   79
7   Before You Begin Writing   91
8   Your First Draft   103
9   Adding Ease to Your Writing Process   125
10   What to Know About Editing   145

PART 3: PUBLISHING   159

11   Your Publishing Needs, Wants, and Desires   161
12   Author Beware—Scams   173
13   Author Beware—Censorship   187
14   Picking the Best Publishing Path for You   201
15   What to Ask a Publisher   215
16   Your Publishing Costs   229
17   Your Publishing Timeline   247
18   Your Book Launch + Beyond   257

Conclusion   273

Reader Resources   281
About Jenn   287
Hire Jenn to Speak   288
Acknowledgments   289
Bibliography   290
The B Corp Movement   291

PREFACE

Dear Reader,

Hi there. Welcome to *Publish Your Purpose*—both this book and my company! My name is Jenn, and this is the story of how I became a book publisher.

In 2012, I was overwhelmed and confused about all of the options in the self-publishing market. I had absolutely no idea what I was doing. None. I began asking friends who had published books about their process, and I slowly cobbled together a plan for myself.

As an LGBTQ+ consultant in the financial services and insurance industries, I had clients asking me, "Jenn, when are you going to write a book?" I had conference planners saying, "Jenn, we'd love to be able to include a book for our audience when we have you here to speak." And I had potential clients saying, "Do you have a book so I can get a sense of your approach before we move forward?"

It was a wake-up call. Not only did *I* feel like I needed to write a book, but everyone I was serving was *also* telling me that I needed to write a book.

Throughout 2012 and into 2013, I assembled the team I needed to self-publish my first book, *But You Don't Look Gay: 6 Steps in Creating a Successful LGBT Marketing Strategy*. It worked! My hard work and endless hours of research and planning paid off.

I Didn't Know What I Didn't Know

Regardless of my planning, I didn't put my best foot forward. There were so many things I didn't know that I needed to know, that I unintentionally shortcutted some of the steps and had a subpar book to show for it. It wasn't my fault. As a first-time author, I had no way of fully understanding the process involved in becoming a smashing success. My book still sold and my clients appeared happy, but I didn't feel comfortable putting all my marketing expertise behind it because it didn't live up to my, albeit perfectionist, standards.

Amazon Bestseller on My Second Attempt

In 2014, I took all of my knowledge from the first book I published and wrote and published my second book, *No Wait...You Do Look Gay! The 7 Mistakes Preventing You from Selling to the $830 Billion LGBT Market*. That process was *much* smoother! My hard work and experience showed, and this one sold twice as fast, climbing the ranks to Amazon bestseller status without nearly as much effort. (It was still a lot of work, but I was better prepared—more on that later in this book.) I was proud of the outcome.

The Rise to (Industry) Thought Leader

In the middle of 2015, people in my network began asking if they could "pick my brain" on how I self-published my first two books. I had dozens upon dozens of coffee dates and shared everything I had learned. I was passing along my knowledge because those in my network were kind enough to pass along theirs to me when I needed it.

Midway through 2015 I published a third book, *Marriage Equality Marketing: 5 Questions You Must Ask to Sell to the $884 Billion LGBT Market*. This time it was in celebration of LGBTQ+ marriage equality passing in the United States, a deeply relevant topic to the consulting work I was doing. It was also a different experience because I did it exclusively as an ebook. This ebook was fantastic for growing my mailing list, attracting new clients for consulting engagements, and getting folks to hire me as a speaker more often. This was a life-changing moment of triumph for me!

Toward the end of 2015, I was part of a group coaching program and brought this up somewhat casually: "You know, a lot of amazing people I know are looking to write and publish their books, and I found a formula that works. What if I were to try to teach others how to do it?"

My business coach gave me enthusiastic approval and suggested that I "sell it before I create it." These words of wisdom were *the best* I had ever received. When creating an online product (and your book), it's helpful to test the market and see what people are looking for *before* you spend a lot of money producing something, only to find out you missed the mark a bit.

When creating an online product (and your book), it's helpful to test the market and see what people are looking for before you spend a lot of money producing something, only to find out you missed the mark a bit.

On a Mission to Serve

In February 2016, I grabbed seven people close to me and said, "Listen, I know you need this. And I know how to do this. But I'm not sure how I'm going to execute this yet. If you aren't 100 percent happy with how the next three months unfold, I'll give you all of your money back, no questions asked." I got seven yeses instantly. (And not one asked for their money back.)

This was the birth of what is now our "Getting Started for Authors" program (which has taken many names since it was first created). I was in this to help the amazing people I knew broaden their messages. I had an epiphany, and it was BIG: *What if I were the engine behind the scenes helping other thought leaders get their messages out to the world—and earning up to $22,000 per speaking engagement or more while doing it?*

At this point, I was getting paid an average of $15,000 per speaking engagement. I felt amazing and on top of the world. There's no greater high than walking out to a packed room of people wanting to hear my message. I still feel amazing when I speak to a crowd.

But I wanted to IMPACT more people. More speaking engagements sounded great, but the heavy travel demands of a professional public speaker didn't jive with what I wanted from my life. My aha moment came out of the blue: *What if I were to help other people reach the point where they too can stand in front of a crowd of five thousand people and share their message?*

I knew being a published author was a huge part of my ability to increase my speaking fees. I started at $1,000 in early 2012. After I published my first book, I jumped to $2,500. Then I realized I was short-changing myself and jumped to $5,000 shortly after. I kept raising my fees, and corporations and event organizers kept saying yes! My highest-paid speaking engagement in early 2017 was $22,000.

But back to the impact.

Me standing in front of an audience of five thousand is great for the audience—and great for my bottom line. But me helping countless (or even 10) thought leaders share their message to an audience of five thousand increases my impact by 10! And that was if I served just 10 people. My visions and present-day impact far exceed that.

I could feel it in my bones. *This* is what I was meant to be doing for a living.

I loved my consulting clients, and I loved making the world a better place for LGBTQ+ people through that consulting work. But me behind the scenes, in the driver's seat, pushing incredible people into the spotlight to change the world for the better, is where I was born to be.

My area of expertise for over 15 years was LGBTQ+ in the workplace. But my interests go well beyond that. I want equality for *everyone*, not just the LGBTQ+ community, and not just for the more obvious ways that that might show up. But I quickly saw that my area of expertise didn't necessarily mean it was my superpower.

But you know what *is* my superpower? Helping others get in front of the right audience because they are published experts in their fields. Then *they* can impact the world in ways I personally am unable to.

This shows up in everything that I do and everything we do at Publish Your Purpose (PYP). We work to elevate voices from all diverse communities who have faced any number of adversities in their lives. As non-fiction book publishers, this isn't our sole focus. But if you look at our catalog of books, you'll see common themes of people using their personal, sometimes tragic, experiences to pave the way and make the path better for someone behind them.

This is my life's purpose and why I exist. I *need* to help people tell the stories that other publishers may not want to tell or be passionately committed to telling. We need to hear voices from *all* communities of people so we can learn, share, and grow as human beings and leave the world a better place than we found it.

PYP's First Book in Eight Months

After a successful first run of coaching those initial seven people on how to publish their books in early 2016, I ran the program three more times that year and made significant overhauls to the curriculum as I went. We still make routine updates because there are always better and more efficient ways of doing things that we want to share with you.

In August of 2016, I had only been doing this officially for six months when one of my students said, "Jenn, I really think you need to start a publishing company—and be the one who produces these books for people."

He had planted a seed.

I *could* be the one who brings these stories to life—and help these inspiring people take their stories and messages to the individual communities they're looking to inspire and impact.

It was a win-win-win.

I was hesitant.

I had NO idea how to start, let alone run a publishing company. But I knew how to start my consulting company, grow a speaker business, and publish my own books.

Most importantly, I knew how to TEACH—how to show people exactly what they should do to follow in my footsteps and see the success of publishing their thought leadership.

After hemming and hawing for less than two weeks, I sprung out of bed one morning and declared to the universe, "Alright, we are doing this! Let's go!" Challenge accepted.

I had *not* set out to start a publishing company. It came to me. It was meant to be.

On April 25, 2017, eight months after the initial seed was planted that I should start a publishing company, PYP published our first book.

We then published 12 books in our first year.

Sometimes I still have to pinch myself when I look back and see what I've accomplished as an individual and what my company has accomplished as a team.

Avoid First-Time Author Mistakes

I knew there had to be a better way to help authors along the journey of publishing a book. I had heard so many horror stories of bad publishing experiences that I set out to ensure that PYP is different—and that we remain different. My personal core mission, and subsequently a large part of PYP's core focus, is to protect. We're protecting you from a terrible first-time publishing experience. You don't know what you don't know, and we know that. We want to help you navigate through that rather than take advantage of you, as many do in this industry.

You Are Good Enough

Do any of these sound familiar?

- "Who am I to write a book? No one wants to hear my story."
- "Someone else has already written something similar."
- "I want to write my story, but I'm not a writer."
- "Who's going to care about what I have to say?"
- "I'm sure other people can do this better than me."

We invite you to come with *all* of your baggage. We won't judge you.

You are *not* alone. I've written and published seven (including this one) of my own books. But guess what? As I have written the book that you're holding in your hand, I've had these same doubts swirling in my head.

This is what makes us all human.

Please keep me posted on your progress and successes as you get your book written and published. You can contact me anytime at jgrace@publishyourpurpose.com.

Onward to your reading adventure!

INTRODUCTION

> First forget inspiration. Habit is more dependable. Habit will sustain you whether you're inspired or not. Habit will help you finish and polish your stories. Inspiration won't. Habit is persistence in practice. —Octavia Butler

The file for this book that you're holding in your hands started on July 9, 2020. It's a file I went back and opened about a dozen times, with a pattern of revisiting this book project in the summer.

I knew I would write this book; I was just waiting for the exact moment of inspiration to strike because I knew that time would come. It's something I often tell my authors or those who aspire to become one. If I could capture the lightning in a bottle for when the timing is just perfect, I'd be a billionaire. But that's not how this process works.

So in this book, we're going to cover the essentials, the foundation, and the must-know items to start you on your path of publishing *your* purpose. It's a formula I've followed for myself over and over again, and something I've taught hundreds of others to do as well. The common through line you'll find throughout this book is the importance of approaching this entire process strategically.

Your Story

Let's start with the question that you've probably been asking yourself the entire time you've had this book project on your mind: *Is my story worth telling?*

That's a confronting question, isn't it? And you might be asking yourself, *Did she really just call me out like that in the introduction of her book?*

Yes. Yes, I did.

Why? Because I *know* your story is worth telling.

Here's the deal.

There is someone out there who *needs* to hear your story. They need to hear your unique perspective. To feel hope. To feel a sense of belonging. Knowing that the path you've traveled is now a road that can lead your readers to better experiences and outcomes is priceless.

Your experiences have led you to where you are. You have the power to shortcut the journey for those who are looking to do so. It's up to you to gather the courage to share your process, methodology, framework—and most importantly, *your story*.

This is scary stuff. It's a big responsibility.

Think of the last person who said to you, "You really should write a book." Without being creepy, I want you to print a picture of that person and put it on your monitor. I want you to sit down and write. And write with just that ONE person in mind. Write your book for them and them alone. Even if you only write for one hour this week, that's one hour closer to having your book written.

Why You Need to Tell Your Story

The first big hurdle in your journey to authorship is to finally take the plunge and dedicate yourself to writing your book. You're here and reading this, so we can check the first big hurdle off the list.

However, the second hurdle, which can be even harder to overcome than the first, is the puzzlement about what kind of book is best for you to write. In my daily conversations with people, the question of what type of book I'm writing always comes up.

At Publish Your Purpose (yes, my company name and the name of this book are the same, intentionally), the vast majority of the books we've published fall into a hybrid that I like to call a "Non-fiction/Memoir Blend." It's not a sexy name, but it's accurate and is exactly as it sounds: a non-fiction book that has your story intentionally woven into the subject that you're teaching your readers about.

As thought leaders, we can become unsettled to share our stories when we're so accustomed to teaching what we know, not who we are. If you approach this from a strategic lens, the payoff will be tenfold.

It's been suggested that readers recall approximately 50 percent more information from stories than from data presented on its own.[1] Professor Chip Heath presented two speeches to his students at Stanford University. After only 10 minutes, 63 percent of the students could recall the stories told in the speech, but only 5 percent were able to recollect any single statistic mentioned.[2] Stories are proven to be how people remember information.

You may be questioning the relevancy of your story as it relates to something you're teaching. As thought leaders, we can become unsettled to share our stories when we're so accustomed to teaching what we know, not who we are. If you approach this from a strategic lens, the payoff will be tenfold.

There are many benefits to leveraging your story within your book, below are just a few. When considering to what degree you want to share your story, think about the following benefits and how they may relate to the goals of your book (more about your goals in Chapter 2):

1. **Your story can have an important impact.**

    Your story allows you to impact your audience on both an individual and a population-wide level. Sharing your life story can make someone with a similar experience or background feel seen, understood, and a little less alone in this world, which is a very powerful thing. Publishing your story can not only help others feel represented but also lead your audience to stand up and speak up about their own lives.

    Here are some other questions to ask yourself when deciding whether a story can have a valuable impact on your audience:

    - Are there lessons learned in my life that could be valuable toward shaping the lives of my audience?

---

[1] A. C. Graesser, M. Singer, and T. Trabasso, "Constructing Inferences During Narrative Text Comprehension," *Psychological Review* 101, no. 3(1994): 371–395, https://doi.org/10.1037/0033-295x.101.3.371.

[2] Chip Heath and Dan Heath, *Made to Stick* (New York: Random House, 2007).

🔖 Does my story have insights that could inspire personal reflection or revelation in my readers?

🔖 Could people who have different beliefs than me gain a new perspective on the world through reading about my experiences?

2. **Telling your story allows you to connect on a deeper level with your network.**

The etiquette expected in the professional world can sometimes make it difficult to connect on a personal level to the people around you. Telling your story within your book is one solution to this issue because it tells the story of you; it allows people to have a new understanding of who you are and what you stand for. If you haven't been able to talk about your history or how you got to where you are as an expert, your book can cover the basics for you.

Your experiences are also great talking points that open the door for new conversations. In addition, this is an act of vulnerability and can demonstrate a willingness to be open. Letting down your walls in your writing signals to others that you're able to have real conversations that go beyond small talk. Meaningful conversations forge emotional connections, in turn strengthening your relationships, which can further your goals for this book and your work at large.

3. **Your story allows you to explore yourself and your past in new ways.**

We're all shaped and changed by a lifetime of experiences and interactions. Sometimes diving into just your professional story or your innovations isn't enough to truly demonstrate who you are or what you want to teach your readers. Going deep with your personal story allows room to include smaller, but necessary details, giving readers an even clearer understanding of your motivations and values.

Also, your story can reveal personal truths to more than just your readers. Writing your story requires confronting your past and closely analyzing how each moment in your life has impacted you. Working through previous emotions may bring clarity or relief in unexpected ways. The journey can also be very rewarding because you can trace your growth clearly and see how far you've come. When you lay out your story on paper, you can see the progress you've made in a way you couldn't when you were still in it.

Your story can provide both emotional and professional triumphs and is a very direct way to meaningfully impact your desired audience. Being 100 percent honest and completely vulnerable is never easy—and will probably be very difficult at times—but through the writing process, you're doing yourself and your audience a great service that will change your lives for the better.

Your Fear

Having just spent time diving into *why* you need to tell your story, I can almost predict where your mind is at right now: fear.

You may have a little trepidation, or you might be on the edge of a panic attack. Wherever you fall in this spectrum, it's okay and normal to feel this way. Writing a book does something that no other form of content or communication does—it exposes you to being fully seen. Being seen can be confronting, it can be scary, and it can be overwhelming. We've all read or heard the statistic that most people fear public speaking more than death.[3] I think writing a book comes pretty close here too.

But I want to express to you the absolute power to be harnessed in being seen. Being seen can show up in a myriad of ways. If you're like me, perhaps you know how defeating it can be when you walk into a room and you are

---

3 Pat Ladouceur, "What We Fear More Than Death," MentalHelp.net, accessed March 7, 2023, https://www.mentalhelp.net/blogs/what-we-fear-more-than-death/.

INTRODUCTION

- the *only* LGBTQ+ person,
- the *only* person of color,
- the *only* woman, or
- the *only* person with a disability.

I'm routinely the *only* LGBTQ+ person in a room, and quite often the *only* woman. I'm used to this. And you may be too. But do you know what also comes with being the *only*? More responsibility and more pressure.

The biggest fears people have related to their book include,

- What if my book sucks?
- What if I'm an embarrassment? and
- What if my book is a raging success?

But as someone who is an *only*, this can often be an even bigger fear. At PYP, we work with established business owners, entrepreneurs, professionals, speakers, and those just starting out. And guess what? Every single one of them has expressed this fear.

I'm not immune either. As I've launched my own books, I've felt the same paralyzing fear—that it will be terrible and will do more damage to my brand than good. We'll cover this in more detail in Chapter 4 when we talk about imposter syndrome.

It's good to have a healthy amount of fear because this pushes us outside of our comfort zones. But allowing this to become bigger than it needs to be will have a crippling effect. Worst of all, it will affect the impact you'll have on the world through your thought leadership.

You and those you serve can't afford for you *not* to tell your story. If you take the writing of your book one step at a time, I promise it will be something you can be proud of. Stop thinking about yourself, and start thinking about those who need to hear your message.

Pay close attention to the picture of the person you have hanging on your monitor as inspiration. Remember them. Remember *why* you're writing your book. If you follow the steps outlined in this book, you can put your fear right back in its place and continue on this incredible and rewarding journey.

> Writing a book does something that no other form of content or communication does—it exposes you to being fully seen.

Commit To Yourself

Now's the time to make a commitment to yourself. To show yourself that *you* can do this. That *you* have what it takes to get your book written and published.

The first of many things I'm asking of you is to sign a contract with yourself. This book is filled with opportunities to engage personally. I've also created a workbook that you can get at www.PublishYourPurpose.com/book-extras to follow along with ease.

Go grab the workbook and open the "Contract with Myself" document. I want you to then hang it somewhere visible. Somewhere where you'll see it regularly. We've had authors post it on their refrigerators, in their bathrooms, and on the visors of their cars. It's going to be an ongoing source of inspiration and a reminder that you're meant to put your vision and purpose into the world.

BOTTOM LINE: You Can Do This!

When times get tough and you doubt why you're writing this book, think of who you're doing this for. Keep putting one foot in front of the other. I promise, you *will* make progress! This book is going to give you a roadmap that will help you find your footing, put one foot in front of the other, and have an amazing quality book of your own at the end of this process—without it totally consuming your life.

I, like you, don't have time to isolate myself in a cabin in the woods for six months to write a book. Yet I've been able to find pockets of time over the last decade to write seven books, including the one you're reading. Writing and publishing a book are both team sports, which you'll learn as you read on.

I'm all about efficiency as a human, but I'm also about strategy. I want your book to be a strategic work of art, but I want you to find an efficient path to get there. We're all busy with our professions, businesses, and families, so being able to get your book written within a reasonable time frame without negatively impacting your life is my goal for you.

PUBLISH YOUR PURPOSE

One of my favorite quotes is from Neale Donald Walsh, who said, "Life begins at the edge of your comfort zone."[4] I'm going to ask you to take a leap with me throughout this book, and I promise you it'll be a rewarding one.

Now, grab your favorite beverage, a pen, and a piece of paper, and let's start creating a plan.

---

4   Neale Donald Walsh, *Conversations with God: An Uncommon Dialogue* (London, Hodder & Stoughton, 1997).

GROW
FURTHER

Download the Publish Your Purpose workbook so that you can follow along and see your plan physically take shape on the pages in front of you. I promise it'll be worth it!

Access the workbook here:
https://publishyourpurpose.com/book-extras.

PROMOTE YOUR PURPOSE

Throughout this book you'll find that each chapter is separated by a marketing moment. Strategy is one of the most important parts of the book writing and publishing processes, so in order to be strategic we need to think about the future.

Too often, authors wait until their book is fully written to begin marketing their book. I do not want this for you. Therefore, between chapters, you'll find a simple marketing idea that you can explore while you're writing your manuscript.

PART 1: MINDSET

Welcome to Part 1: Mindset. The following chapters are going to help us set the foundation for your journey of becoming an author. Rather than diving right into the writing process, we're going to first talk about your purpose, your impact, and your vision, then we'll tackle your personal and professional goals for your book. We'll dive into getting in the right mindset and then round it all out by covering the best ways to hold yourself accountable. If you put your mind to this, you *will* succeed. You just need the right tools to get there, which we're about to cover!

CHAPTER 1
Your Purpose, Vision, and Impact, Oh My!

When Publish Your Purpose (PYP) was founded in late 2015/early 2016, we chose to put purpose at the forefront of everything that we do, every author that we work with, and every stakeholder we communicate with. In every decision that we make, purpose is at the core.

Purpose is a core value of our publishing company for both its internal meaning and its external meaning. According to Dictionary.com, purpose as a noun means, "the reason for which something exists or is done, made, used, etc." or "an intended or desired result; end; aim; goal."[5]

Our mission at PYP is to elevate the voices often excluded from traditional publishing by intentionally seeking out authors and storytellers with diverse backgrounds, life experiences, and unique perspectives that will make an impact in the world. We believe in free speech, the ability to walk down the street without harassment or persecution, and leaving the environment better than when we found it. As a hybrid publisher, we wear our mission and values on our sleeves proudly so that we ensure we're working with authors who also share those values.

When your purpose is front and center in what you do, specifically throughout the writing and publishing processes of your book, I promise you that the process will become exponentially easier as a result. It doesn't mean it won't have moments of being hard or difficult, but what it does

---

5 Dictionary.com, s.v. "purpose (*n.*)," accessed March 7, 2023, https://www.dictionary.com/browse/purpose.

mean is that you have something to fall back into, align with, lean on, and anchor onto.

This chapter is going to dive into two equally important topics: not just the *purpose* of your book but also the *vision* for it. Having a clear sense of both of these will keep you moving when times get tough and you want to quit before you've finished your book.

Why Purpose Needs to be at the Forefront of Your Book and Writing

When writing your book, there needs to be intention and purpose behind the words that you're putting down on paper. You need to align your priorities and goals. If you're writing a book with the explicit purpose of trying to make the most amount of money without any regard for impact or purpose, there's a high probability that your book will fail. Writing a book is a grueling process that requires dedication and time—going from an idea in your head to a fully fleshed-out book requires a lot of effort.

Writing a book can be a long process. For some it may take months, and for others it may take years—and in some instances, decades. Getting to a first draft poses a challenge for many. Depending on how you're publishing your book, you also need to determine the layout, book design, and marketing. All of these take more time and can leave you exhausted and unmotivated to finish your book. This is where your purpose comes in.

Writing is an emotional process. Writing about certain topics that pertain to your life, or recounting life experiences, can trigger deep emotional responses that may make you want to shy away from writing. Dealing with author blues and also thinking about how much further you have to go before you're finished can leave you thinking, *Why the hell did I even start writing this?*

This is when you or someone else can remind you of the purpose of why you're writing this book in the first place. The stronger that purpose is, the stronger the motivator you have to push through those low moments and keep going. If you're writing to impact the lives of others, thinking about how people's lives will be changed can keep you going, even in the roughest of times.

> When your purpose is front and center in what you do, specifically throughout the writing and publishing processes of your book, I promise you that the process will become exponentially easier as a result.

When you have a purpose behind what you're doing, there's also a dedication to finish writing. If writing isn't your chosen profession and you're working 40+ hours a week while balancing a family, hobbies, and everything else, it can be hard to set aside an hour a day or on a weekend to sit in front of a computer screen and write. Keeping yourself motivated can be hard and making the time for it can be even harder. This is why it takes many people years to finish the first draft of their manuscript. Even if it does take years, those who are dedicated to finishing their drafts have a strong sense of purpose behind writing it in the first place—and they know that once it's out into the world it'll have their desired impact.

Finding Your Purpose

What if you don't know what your purpose is? What if you feel your purpose is too surface-level? I encourage you to go to www.PublishYourPurpose.com/book-extras and download the free workbook that goes with this book. There you'll find the following purpose exercise that you can write alongside. You're also welcome to write right in this book, but please know I'll be cringing from a distance knowing you're writing here.

Take this time to center yourself in *your* why, the why you've chosen to write and publish a book. Your answers don't need to be solely outwardly focused on others, so think about yourself here too.

To make this exercise a little easier, here are a couple of starter examples I've heard throughout running our free Publish Your Purpose Author Lab workshop. This is a free multi-day workshop that PYP runs a couple of times a year. I encourage you to check out the most recent replays by going here: www.publishyourpurpose.com/author-lab:

- Jennifer overcame the odds of poverty and housing displacement as a child to build a real estate empire with an intentional focus on giving back to the communities from which she originally came.
- Max is writing their book to help LGBTQ+ individuals heal alongside their family members by navigating them safely through the coming out process.

- Jack lost a child and works with parents who feel broken and are finding themselves again on the other side of loss.
- Adrianne has been living with a chronic illness for a long time and attributes their ability to do so to the encouragement of others. They are writing their book to inspire others so that they can be successful while managing a chronic illness.

What's Your Why?

Reminder: Visit www.PublishYourPurpose.com/book-extras to download the free workbook that goes with this book.

Below are a series of questions to answer. Don't stop at the surface; ask yourself the question two more times to help you get to the deeper answer. This will help you uncover your purpose in a more meaningful way. If you feel there's more to be excavated, keep asking yourself why until you've really gotten to the root.

1. **Why are you writing this book?**
   But why?
   Okay, but why?

2. **Why is it important to put your story into the form of a published book?**
   But why?
   Okay, but why?

3. **Why does this book matter in *your* life?**
   But why?
   Okay, but why?

4. **Why does this book matter in your *readers'* lives?**
   But why?
   Okay, but why?

5. **Why are you committed to making this book a reality?**
   But why?
   Okay, but why?

How are you feeling now that you've answered these questions? Do you have more clarity? Are you feeling lighter? Maybe you're still feeling a little bit overwhelmed because this is the first time you've really dug into these concepts. That's okay. This book is going to hold your hand throughout the process so that you feel safe and supported from start to finish.

The answers you've written either here or in the workbook will help you shine a light on your North Star. This will act as your compass as you move forward through all other aspects of the book writing and publishing processes. If you need to revisit this exercise, do it as many times as it takes for you to feel comfortable and aligned with your true purpose.

Being Centered

When you begin to think about your why, you might see that your why is centered around one (or more) of the following:

- To inspire others
- To change the world
- To help others feel seen or heard
- To make a leap into a new career or industry
- To build a consulting practice
- To become a thought leader

Your why might be wrapped in one of these reasons, all of these reasons, or none of these reasons. Spend some time thinking through other potential reasons why this is so important and meaningful to you.

My core why for the last non-fiction book I wrote, *Beyond the Rainbow*,[6] was to provide a literal bookend to my consulting career. I had written three other books on the topic, and before I closed my consulting business for good I wrote my final book on LGBTQ+ consulting to share the last

---

6 Jenn T. Grace, *Beyond the Rainbow: Personal Stories and Practical Strategies to Help your Business & Workplace Connect with the LGBTQ Market* (Hartford, CT: Publish Your Purpose Press, 2017), https://publishyourpurpose.com/books/beyond-the-rainbow-personal-stories-and-practical-strategies-to-help-your-business-workplace-connect-with-the-lgbtq-market/

remaining insights related to my previous decade of work. The benefit to me was that once I shared my thought leadership in that final book form, I could say, *I've given it my all. I've shared everything in my head that I can with the world.* And my end goal for all of this was to shut down that consulting business and move my energy and focus into solely publishing the books of others.

My core why for my memoir, *House on Fire*,[7] was to help other people feel seen and heard. What I've personally gone through isn't necessarily unique to me, but the number of things that happened in a concentrated period of time *was* unique. Therefore, my singular goal was to put my story out there so any other family who found themselves in a similar situation could feel seen, validated, and less alone.

In my non-fiction books, I always had very clear objectives for what I wanted them to do for my readers, my business, and me. With my memoir, I only had one of these determined: what this book would do for my readers. I approached my memoir with the thought, *I'm going to let my book tell me what it wants me to do. I'm not going to tell it what I want it to do.* This was a far departure from my usual approach and what I teach others to do on a daily basis, but for this particular book, it's what made sense for me.

When I allowed my memoir to tell me what it wanted, I found myself engaging in conversations with multiple book clubs, sharing my experience, and impacting those readers' lives. But the one conversation that made every ounce of effort worthwhile was the one I had with a woman in Indiana, who cried on the phone with me for 45 minutes sharing that, for the very first time, she saw herself and her family reflected in the pages of a book. It was an emotional conversation for both of us because my true purpose was to help even one family feel less alone, and this conversation came just two months after my book had been published. I knew at that moment—in that conversation—that my book was doing exactly what it needed to do in this world. And there is no greater feeling.

---

[7] Jenn T. Grace, *House on Fire* (Hartford, CT: Publish Your Purpose Press, 2020), https://publishyourpurpose.com/books/house-on-fire-finding-resilience-hope-and-purpose-in-the-ashes/.

I share these as examples that you can take into consideration. You must do what feels right for you, which may be different from what is right for the person sitting next to you. What someone else's purpose or why is, what they are doing, will be different from yours. That doesn't make your purpose or why any less valuable or important.

The ultimate goal here is to help you gain clarity so that you have something to lean into when times get tough. Because they will get tough. Your writing will ebb and flow. You'll have moments of difficulty and find that you don't have as much time to work on this as you thought you did. If you can anchor back to why you're doing this, it's going to really increase your chances of crossing the finish line with a published book in hand.

Your Vision

Now that we've scratched the surface of the purpose and why of your book, let's dive into your vision.

I often ask an aspiring author, "If you could wave a magic wand and have your book be available today, what is your book doing for you and what is it doing for your readers?" The answers I hear are wide-ranging. They are both inward facing (how the book will improve their lives) and outward facing (how the book will improve the lives of their readers).

Similar to uncovering your purpose, you may not have a clear vision yet—and that's okay. We're on this journey together, and throughout these next pages we'll work together to elevate this discussion further to think through the vision for your book. I encourage you to go to www.PublishYourPurpose.com/book-extras and download the free workbook that contains this exercise on vision.

Your Vision: Your Life

When I ask you about your vision, I don't just mean your book. Look at your life in general. What energy do you hope your book will bring to your life? What do you want your life to look like in 5 years, 10 years, or 20 years? Can this book help you get there? Do you imagine yourself retired on the beach? Mentoring as a hobby? Spending time with your grandkids?

Do you have wealth and a lot of homes? Do you have a small environmental footprint and relish in solitude?

Really sit and think about what this looks like for you. If you're struggling with envisioning your future, please know you're not alone. It's taken me many years in therapy to get to a place where I can truly dream of my future and not be mired down in daily fight-or-flight mode. If this is you, spend some time with a friend or loved one and brainstorm with them what you imagine your future to look like.

Don't overcomplicate this. Write from the heart. Write what you desire for yourself and your readers. Be creative and don't be shy. No one needs to see this unless you want them to, so be honest about your desires. Don't get stuck on whether you feel like this is right, perfect, or doable—just write it down without judging yourself.

Your Vision: Your Business

What do you want your book to do for your business? Can your book help you get there? Do you want to be the next Brené Brown? Do you want to be known as *the* leading thought leader in your space? Do you want your book to catapult your consulting career? Are you hoping the outcomes of your book will help you on your road to a comfortable retirement?

When you think about what a book can do for your business, the possibilities are endless. You may consider starting a podcast, creating an online program, starting a speaker career, or creating a new product, service, or widget. A strategically written book can be the starting point for all of those amazing revenue-generating opportunities.

Where are you living? Where are your offices located? What hours do you want to work? What type of people do you want to work with? What kind of customers do you want to work with? Do you want to have employees? If so, what kind of people will they be? How much family time will you have in relation to your business? How much profit will your business generate?

These are all really important questions to think about that you may not have the answers for right now—and that's okay. The point of this chapter is to help you think bigger and more expansively, to create space for your book to live.

> Your audience is reading your writing for a reason, and they will leave having learned something.

If your book aligns with your life and your business in a strategic way, you'll be able to have all of these things in harmony. You'll have more clarity, and you'll know where you're headed and how you'll best serve your readers, your audience, and your followers.

Regardless of what you're writing about, for any writing that you put out into the public eye, your readers will be impacted by your work. Your audience is reading your writing for a reason, and they will leave having learned something new or received a deeper understanding of a subject.

Your Vision: Your Impact

Awareness of the impact or impression that you want readers to walk away with will help you formulate your writing in a way that meets your goals. Perhaps in your book you want to talk about your experiences in a work environment, with the main takeaway being to encourage your readers to stand up for themselves in certain situations. You want to use these experiences to offer up guidance for readers, with the intention that when they encounter a similar situation, your book will have impacted their reaction.

There may be times of self-doubt about your writing or a loss of interest in the topic that you're writing about. Knowing that there are people who will be impacted by your writing, or knowing that what you write about is something that needs to be addressed in your community, will help you push through those low points and get your writing finished. When you write your story and speak your truth, you will make an impact.

> "I'm writing this book because we all deserve to have a job that we enjoy."
> —Nancy

> "I'm writing this book because two families in my hometown lost children to suicide."
> —James

Take a look at some of the reader reviews for a few of the books *PYP* has helped bring to life:

PUBLISH YOUR PURPOSE

From *Empathy Is Not a Weakness: And Other Stories from the Edge* by Loren J. Sanders:[8]

Kixsombut

★★★★★ Critical Management Read: how to lead effectively and to just do better
Reviewed in the United States us on February 21, 2023
Verified Purchase

This book should become the next management reading staple. Like "Who Moved My Cheese," the messages in "Empathy Is Not A Weakness," are almost obvious and essential for working people who don't live and work in a bubble, but critical to express and is absorbed differently when read from a book. This book is actually not just for people in management to read, but also for anyone who works with others. Loren Sanders opens up about her own failures as a leader and writes about how she overcomes them, learns from her mistakes and teaches how to do better. From a non-management position, it can reveal the short-sidedness of management and provide an alternative way to manage upwards. Buy, read this book, practice it, and read it again.

From *Self-Elected: How to Put Justice Over Profit and Soar in Business* by Lisa Wise:[9]

Lucy

★★★★★ read this book.
Reviewed in the United States us on February 8, 2023
Verified Purchase

I don't often write reviews, but you should read this book. I own a business, and this book has changed the way I think about the relationship between social justice and business. In schools and organizations, we're taught that social justice is the right thing to do, but that businesses often need to pay a price (i.e., make less profit) to do the right thing. lisa wise flips this thinking on its head and argues convincingly that social justice and business are inextricably linked and move in the same direction. Building a business focused on social justice actually leads to more profits, not less. When you build a purpose-driven organization and invest in people, everyone wins. I'm excited to implement some new ideas in my business and my life after reading this book. Would strongly recommend.

---

8   Loren J. Sanders, *Empathy Is Not a Weakness: And Other Stories from the Edge* (Hartford, CT: Publish Your Purpose Press, 2022), https://publishyourpurpose.com/authors/loren-j-sanders/.

9   Lisa Wise, *Self-Elected: How to Put Justice Over Profit and Soar in Business* (Hartford, CT: Publish Your Purpose Press, 2022), https://publishyourpurpose.com/authors/lisawise/.

From *From Changing Diapers to Changing the World: Why Moms Make Great Advocates and How to Get Started* by Cynthia Changyit Levin:[10]

Jennifer

⭐⭐⭐⭐⭐ **An amazing guide for anyone who wants to make a difference!**
Reviewed in the United States us on March 3, 2022
Verified Purchase

The author has created a book that every parent (or anyone) who wants to create change in the world should read! It is an interactive tool that provides readers with actions for every level of engagement. Her thoughtful examples and real life stories give a full picture of just how easy it can be to get involved to be part of the change you might want to see. As a parent we often wonder "what can I do" or "how do I get involved" - well, Levin gives you answers to those questions along with steps to actually make it happen. She isn't just referring to large campaigns or huge time commitments (she does touch on that) but she is talking about meaningful actions that make a world of difference without spending extra time that you might not feel you have available - to whatever organization(s) you decide to support. Her honest voice and kind spirit come through in her personal outline of how she became an active advocate as a young mother. Her journey is inspirational and will make you smile at the growth you will see in her as she gains confidence in the advocacy world. She has a wealth of information to share and everyone who reads this will benefit from her experience and knowledge.

From *In the Company of Men: How Women can Succeed in a World Built Without Them* by Eileen Scully:[11]

Mary C

⭐⭐⭐⭐⭐ **Fascinating Profiles on Inspiring Unsung She-roes!**
Reviewed in the United States us on January 13, 2020
Verified Purchase

I couldn't put this book down--read it in one sitting! Eileen Scully selected the most amazing and inspirational women to profile--many of them I had never heard of, but truly they should be household names. As you read through the stories of the women and the challenges they took on, there are so many terrific lessons to learn and emulate. I find myself still thinking about this book and how I can be more of a leader and advocate in my own community on issues that matter. I especially love the helpful tips at the end of the book on how to set out to make things happen....truly 5 plus stars! A great book to gift to strong and powerful women (and men) in your life! I will save to pass on to my son when he gets older.

---

10   Cynthia Changyit Levin, (Hartford, CT: Publish Your Purpose Press, 2022), https://publishyourpurpose.com/authors/cynthia-changyit-levin/.

11   Eileen Scully, *In the Company of Men: How Women Can Succeed in a World Built Without Them* (Hartford, CT: Publish Your Purpose Press, 2019), https://publishyourpurpose.com/authors/eileen-scully/.

PUBLISH YOUR PURPOSE

From *I'll Be Right There: A Guidebook for Adults Caring for their Aging Parents* by Fern Pessin:[12]

jordana

★★★★★ A must have for every family, allows you to have those difficult conversations before it's too late
Reviewed in the United States us on September 15, 2019
This book has been life-changing I have cared for my father and currently my husband both with serious illnesses

I wish I had this book when my dad was alive and he still had his cognitive function to assist in all the simple questions of his wishes and detailed information the families argue about because everyone one feels they knew what dad or mom would have wanted. And unfortunately my husband has late stage Alzheimer's and this book wasn't around to help me pre-plan and could've done a lot of things different to help make the financial situation much more comfortable.

Fern helps you discuss the difficult conversations so that the family can Walk together in this journey. Most importantly if you buy the book now and you complete it for yourself you're giving your children a priceless gift because we are a sandwich generation we can use this book as a tool for your own wishes and also use it to help make decisions for our aging parents. Give the gift to our children so they don't have to deal with all stress and aggravation we did because my dad developed a brain tumor which no longer allowed him to make his own decisions.

From *The Multiplier Effect of Inclusion: How Diversity & Inclusion Advances Innovation and Drives Growth* by Dr. Tony Byers:[13]

Kindle Customer

★★★★★ Essential reading for diversity and inclusion leaders
Reviewed in the United States us on September 17, 2019
What a fantastic resource! I have worked in the field of diversity, equity, and inclusion (DEI) for about 15 years and am currently the DEI director of a public housing authority. This book has been an absolute game changer for me and has given me some fantastic tools to help my agency enter into an exciting cultural shift of embracing DEI and undoing institutional racism.

This book was so very accessible and Dr. Byers' expertise and experience was made abundantly clear. Often, we DEI practitioners enter into organizations with a "firefighter" approach of trying to address individual challenges with no thoughtful bigger picture STRATEGY to actually make lasting and meaningful change. This book is more than just wishful thinking and hoping--it provides the road map and the tool set needed to thoughtfully achieve cultural shifts by transforming the ways that we typically think of what diversity is. I plan to read this again with my senior leadership team so that we can all be on the same page and work together towards creating a culture of inclusivity and empowerment. I'm very excited to have read this book and believe that it is essential reading for DEI leaders.

---

12   Fern Pessin, *I'll Be Right There: A Guidebook for Adults Caring for Their Aging Parents* (Hartford, CT: Publish Your Purpose Press, 2019), https://publishyourpurpose.com/authors/fern-pessin/.

13   Tony Byers, *The Multiplier Effect of Inclusion: How Diversity & Inclusion Advances Innovation and Drives Growth* (Hartford, CT: Publish Your Purpose Press, 2018), https://publishyourpurpose.com/authors/dr-tony-byers/.

YOUR PURPOSE, VISION, AND IMPACT, OH MY!

From *Beyond the Rainbow: Personal Stories and Practical Strategies to Help your Business & Workplace Connect with the LGBTQ Market* by Jenn T. Grace:[14]

> JeffB
>
> ★★★★★ Jenn shows how businesses of any size can embrace the LGBTQ community
> Reviewed in the United States us on June 14, 2017
> Jenn provides a valuable look at the assimilation of the LGBTQ community into the workforce and our communities. American businesses are targeting diverse groups like never before largely because of the economic impact. With nearly $1 trillion in buying power, the LGBTQ community rivals other diverse groups and Jenn showcases how businesses of any size can properly embrace the LGBTQ community. Beyond the Rainbow is a powerful book.
> Jeff Berger
> Founder & CEO National Association of Gay & Lesbian Real Estate Professionals (NAGLREP)

As an author, it never gets old seeing a new review come in by a reader whose life has been impacted by your work.

This could be you—and it IS you!

These authors are just like you. They don't have millions of social media followers and they aren't working with giant budgets. They put one foot in front of the other and focused their energy on getting their book written.

When things get hard and you aren't sure what your next step is, remember these three things:

- Who are you doing this for?
- Whose life will be different because you stepped up and shared your story?
- How will your life be different as a published author?

Bottom Line: You Can Do This!

Now, let's get to it! We have a lot to cover in the pages of this book.

---

14 Jenn T. Grace, *Beyond the Rainbow* (Hartford, CT: Publish Your Purpose Press, 2017), https://publishyourpurpose.com/authors/jenn-t-grace/.

GROW FURTHER

Join the Publish Your Purpose Author Lab workshop to take your learning experience offline and into a supportive online group environment where you can discuss your purpose, your vision, and your impact.

Access the workshop here:
https://publishyourpurpose.com/author-lab/.

PROMOTE YOUR PURPOSE

Tell Someone Today

The best way to begin your marketing journey is to tell someone...NOW. Rather than go on this journey alone, tell someone that you're writing this book. Who knows? That someone may become your first book buyer!

If you're unsure who to tell, you can tell me. I'm **@jenntgrace** and **@publishyourpurpose** on social.

CHAPTER 2
Your Goals: Personal, Professional, and Business

Similar to the importance of understanding your purpose, vision, and intended impact, having goals for your book is critical. How you define success for your book is also critical because we can't measure what we can't track.

Goals in all areas of our lives are important to have, but when it comes to a book, having a goal is imperative. As you've already seen from Chapter 1, a lot of hard work goes into creating a book that you can be proud of and that also has the intended impact you're aiming for.

Goal setting is important so that you're setting yourself up with the right expectations. When we approach something without a goal, what are the outcomes? We may achieve some part of the goal, but is it consistent or repeatable? Chances are, no. A strong goal will keep the direction of your book front and center at all times, which wraps around your purpose, impact, and vision.

Goal Setting

Let's think about your goals for this book. Do you want to—

- Be a *New York Times* bestseller?
- Sell one million copies of your book?
- Impact one person?

- Get higher-paid speaking engagements?
- Bring on new consulting/coaching business?

What is *your* goal? The goal that is specific to you. It's not about asking other people for their opinions but sitting down and thinking about your book in particular and how you'll define success on the other side of this process. You could have a goal of your book becoming a bestseller, but if we add metrics around this goal and make it more specific, the chances of us achieving this goal are going to be greater.

Let's talk about SMART goals. You might be familiar with SMART goals already, but let's view this through the lens of writing and publishing your book. SMART is an acronym for specific, measurable, attainable, realistic, and timely. Let's run our bestseller goal through this test:

I want my book to appear on a bestseller list.

- **Is this Specific?**
Yes and no. It's clear that the goal is to get on a bestseller list, but it's not super clear about which bestseller list.

- **Is this Measurable?**
Yes and no. It is in a way because there are some loose metrics around what it takes to be on a bestseller list. But without knowing which list you're aiming for, you may not know how many exact book sales are needed or what else it may take to get there.

- **Is this Attainable?**
Yes and no. If you're aiming to be on an Amazon bestselling list, the answer is yes. There's a clear process to follow to have your book be an Amazon bestseller. If you're aiming to be on the *New York Times* bestseller list, however, that's more like trying to catch lightning in a bottle. It's going to be hard, and attainability is going to depend on you, your platform, and your marketing and sales skills, among other things.

- **Is this Realistic?**
Yes and no. If you're aiming to be on an Amazon bestselling list, the answer is yes, like above. Since there's a clear formula to follow

YOUR GOALS: PERSONAL, PROFESSIONAL, AND BUSINESS

to make this happen, you must spend the time and energy needed to learn that formula (or work with a publisher who can support this). But if you're aiming to be on the *New York Times* bestseller list, it may be trickier. If you have millions of followers with large platforms on social media as well as a big mailing list, then there's a chance that this is a realistic goal for you. But if you don't have a large following or platform, that will likely put this into the unrealistic category.

Is this Timely?

No. This isn't a time-bound goal because it doesn't specify when you'll do this. It could be assumed that this is upon the launch of your book, but the goal doesn't state that specifically. So let's reframe:

OLD GOAL: *I want my book to appear on a bestseller list.*

NEW GOAL: *I want my book to be #1 on the Amazon bestselling list in the Business & Leadership Category, within one week of my book launching.*

NEW GOAL: *I want my book to become a New York Times bestseller as soon as it launches, as I've grown a following of 500,000 people on my mailing list.*

Let's try this with a different kind of goal:

I want my book to make an impact in someone's life.

Is this Specific?

Yes and no. It's specific in the sense that it's stating that you want your book to make an impact, but it doesn't go into depth on what that impact looks like.

Is this Measurable?

No, it's not. There's nothing specifying what period of time this is occurring in, how many people, or how you're defining impact.

🔖 Is this Attainable?
Yes, because it's written as "in someone's life." It's attainable simply because it's broad and can mean a lot of things.

🔖 Is this Realistic?
Yes, but again it feels realistic because it's broad by saying "in someone's life." You haven't declared that the whole world is going to be impacted by this book—now *that* would not be realistic.

🔖 Is this Timely?
No, it's not. There are no parameters around this goal in terms of when this will happen.

OLD GOAL: *I want my book to make an impact in someone's life.*

NEW GOAL: *Within three months of my book launch, I want to have had a conversation with one person who was dramatically impacted by my book.*

Are you starting to get the hang of this idea of goal setting?

Dollars and Cents

If you have a business or are planning on using your book as a way to grow your thought leadership, the next lens of goal setting is putting dollars and cents into your goals.

Our first goal of becoming a bestseller could be based in ego. Our second goal is altruistic and focused on serving. But what about financial goals? Let's think about what some of your financial goals could be for your book. Here are some potentials:

- 🔖 *I want to sell five thousand copies of my book during my launch week, which will net me $35,000 in sales.*
- 🔖 *I want my book to sell enough copies to break even on my $20,000+ investment in publishing my book.*
- 🔖 *I want my book to fuel confidence in me that will help increase my speaker fee.*

> A strong goal will keep the direction of your book front and center at all times, which wraps around your purpose, impact, and vision.

> 🖋 *I want my book to help me get in front of new clients that will help me add six figures in revenue from a new revenue stream.*

When we have clarity on our goals, the sky's the limit in terms of how many books we can sell and how many lives can be impacted.

Similar to our chapter on purpose, we want to always ask *why* multiple times to get to the real goal. This can be a good litmus test that will help identify the validity of our goals. You can work your way through a series of why's and then decide whether the goal is the right fit for you. If you find that it isn't, you can start from the beginning again.

Let's go back to the goal of *I want my book to appear on a bestseller list.*

Why?
I want to have the stature that my book is a bestseller.

Why?
I want the respect and credibility that comes with being a bestseller.

Why?
Because people in my network respect books that have been on bestselling lists—it shows credibility.

Why? (In this case, why is the respect of your peers important?)
Because I want my network to understand how good my work is.

Why?
Because I know my work is good, but I'm not sure they do.

Why?
Because I often think I'm not the best marketer.

Why?
Because I don't have as many sales as I would like to have.

Do you see how this can go on and on and on and on—before getting to a really solid goal? In this fictitious example, the goal looks like it's rooted in appearances and ego, not in purpose and impact. There's nothing wrong with a healthy ego; hell, you need a healthy ego to write a book. But you have to see when and where your ego is really just getting in the way of your purpose, impact, and vision.

Investing In Yourself

Whichever method you use to publish your book, be it traditional, self-publishing, or hybrid publishing (more on this in Chapter 14), having it done right can make your name and your business stand out from the rest. If your book is edited, designed, and marketed properly, you'll see positive returns through your business, high book sales, more leads, higher pay for speaking engagements, and new customers for your business.

It's important to note that this doesn't come from simply writing a book, especially if that book is sloppily written or published. Your book is a representation of you and your brand, and the more you invest in your book, the better the results will be. And not just money-wise. You can spend $5,000 for a book designer to create the graphics, cover, and layout of your book, but just because you're paying top dollar doesn't always mean you're getting top quality—we'll cover this in detail in Chapter 16.

Investing in Your Impact

Investing in your book also means investing your time and energy into writing your book and getting your book idea out of your head and onto paper. Writing a book and organizing your thoughts takes time. You want to make sure that your message and your story are being conveyed clearly and that the lessons and stories that you're trying to tell are told with a purpose. Investing in the right writing team or publishing house, and in your own writing, will ensure that you're publishing top-quality work—and your audience will be able to see that.

As mentioned before, if your intention behind writing is to try and generate the most amount of money possible, then your writing or book will most likely fail. Your readers will connect with your book and your words only when they feel that you put yourself into it. When an author is simply slapping together words on a page to rush it into the marketplace, readers know it. When this happens, it does more damage to your reputation than good.

> Your book is a representation of you and your brand, and the more you invest in your book, the better the results will be.

Giving You Credibility in Your Field

By virtue of having a book published under your name, you become recognized as an expert in your field. By putting your thoughts, experiences, and advice into a book for other people to learn and grow from, you'll be seen as a thought leader who's creating new and innovative ideas about how to tackle certain problems. This also applies to your business. The practices and advice that you put in your book are things that other businesses might look to for improvement in their own processes. Much like a degree from an accredited university, having a published book under your belt makes you and your business stand out from the rest. It demonstrates experience in your field and shows that you have the expert knowledge to change a business or practice for the better.

Opening New Doors and Opportunities

Having more credibility also gives you new chances and opportunities in your field. This can be new speaking engagements or getting your foot in the door with new clients. Having your name and your book out there, and elevated, gives you more publicity and allows you to market yourself and your brand more effectively and on a larger scale. In order to reach those new opportunities, you need to market yourself, your book, and your business effectively. New clients and businesses won't just walk in through the door, not unless you're actively promoting yourself and your book.

Laying the Groundwork for Growing Your Business

With the credibility and new opportunities gained by having a book under your belt and a part of your business brand, you can grow your business; and if you've been speaking or consulting, it can help get your business off the ground. The type of work you do may change and expand depending on what potential clients are requesting from you. You may have started out as a speaker, helping educate businesses or communities and sharing your story, but potential clients may now be asking you to speak at more engagements or consult for them. How well your book performs and, as mentioned, how your book is marketed, will determine how many opportunities you and your business get and how much your business grows from your book.

The Power of *Your* Book

With the understanding that your book is of high quality, let's take it a step further and think through the interconnectedness of your book within your business. One of PYP's superpowers is our strategic vision for how to integrate your book into your business. For a book to live to its full potential, we must think of it as part of a larger ecosystem that's intentionally connected.

In your business currently, do you have the following? Check all that apply:

☐ A product

☐ A service

☐ An online presence

☐ A newsletter

☐ An online course

☐ A workbook

☐ Other thought leadership (white paper/case study)

☐ A podcast

☐ A blog

☐ A (soon to be) book

If you checked more than one of these boxes then it's time to get strategic, if you aren't already.

Have you thought through how any of the above items connect? If you're a service-based business, how is your newsletter or blog connected to your service? Do you have specific calls to action for your clients, customers, or readers? This book will act as your guide for how to strategically place calls to action. Keep an eye out throughout for examples.

Bottom Line: You Can Do This!

As you continue through this book, we're going to discuss how to add an intentional strategic lens to your book so that you're making the maximum impact you can on both your readers and the customers they may eventually turn into.

GROW FURTHER

Join the Publish Your Purpose Author Lab workshop to take your learning experience offline and into a supportive online group environment where you can discuss your personal, professional, and business goals.

Access the workshop here:
https://publishyourpurpose.com/author-lab/.

PROMOTE YOUR PURPOSE

Tell a Group

Promoting and marketing your book requires going outside of your comfort zone. Telling a group of people that you're writing a book will provide accountability, but it also sets the foundation for your future promotional efforts.

It's rare that I would ever advise an author to leave a book to go on social media. In fact, this is the exact opposite advice I would give. But I'm breaking my own rule to really force you outside of your comfort zone and into some real-deal accountability.

I want you to set a timer for 10 minutes, do this activity, then come back.

Go to your social media platform of choice and tell your community that you're writing a book. You're welcome to blame me **@jenntgrace / @publishyourpurpose**.

CHAPTER 3 Getting into the Right Mindset

In this chapter, we're going to explore how to get you into the best mindset possible to achieve your goal of writing and publishing your book. Your mindset is a pivotal piece of the puzzle, as it has the direct ability to make or break the success of this endeavor. I want to first get you to a place of envisioning what your book will look and feel like.

Start With the End in Mind

REMINDER: *Visit www.PublishYourPurpose.com/book-extras to download the free workbook that goes with this book.*

Walt Disney is often credited for the quote, "If you can dream it, you can do it." These words are applicable to what I'd like you to do next. I want you to fully embody what you believe your book will look like, feel like, and smell like.

When we're able to see clearly what our vision is in a three-dimensional way, it brings us that much closer to making our book-writing dream a reality. So let's change things up and start with the end in mind. Let's start by finding inspiration.

Let's Go to the Bookstore

Let's take a trip to the bookstore, shall we? I love going to a good, independent bookstore, but any bookstore will do. If you don't have a bookstore accessible to you, head over to your local library, which will work just as well.

I find this activity to be best done in person, but if you're unable to do so, you can do this by browsing your favorite online retailer. (I'm a super fan of Bookshop.org, which is a B Corp just like PYP, meaning they are meeting the highest standards of environmentally friendly and socially responsible business practices.)

What I want you to do is aimlessly browse the shelves of books and see what books jump out to you. Find a book that you're inspired by. A book that you would be proud to hold in your hand if you were the author of that book. It doesn't have to be about the topic you're writing about, but ideally you'll want to at least find a non-fiction book so that you aren't finding inspiration in a sci-fi or romance book cover that won't have a broader application for you down the road.

When you're looking for inspiration, look at both the cover and the inside design. Find a book that you love wholly, regardless of the topic. Try to find that one book that you're in love with. If you're at the bookstore, buy it. If you're at the library, borrow it. Now, display this book wherever you're writing (more on where to write in Chapter 9). This book will become a source of inspiration for you.

You can take this one step further and wrap the book with your book title and name. Be creative and think like a fourth grader. Grab a couple of sheets of computer paper and tape it around the book you just bought. Write your working title, subtitle, and your name on the front of it. It may look sloppy, but what you have is a book with your book title and name on it, sitting right in front of you. Now, that's inspiration!

Your Mindset

Now that we have a little excitement and a dose of energy-providing inspiration, let's talk about getting into the right mindset. When tackling any big goal, getting your mind in the right place can make or break your success and/or your ability to achieve that particular goal. Writing a book is no different. The number of mental gymnastics we do to start and subsequently finish a project can be extreme.

Rather than your mindset being an afterthought, let's focus on how to make it a priority so that we can ensure you finish your manuscript and, subsequently, publish your book. In the next chapter, we'll discuss what your support system will look like and how to seek accountability when you need it, which will work even better when you're approaching this with the right mindset.

We're All Imposters

Have you heard of the term *imposter syndrome*? Psychology Today defines it this way: "People who struggle with imposter syndrome believe that they are undeserving of their achievements and the high esteem in which they are, in fact, generally held. They feel that they aren't as competent or intelligent as others might think—and that soon enough, people will discover the truth about them. Those with imposter syndrome are often well accomplished; they may hold high office or have numerous academic degrees."[15] Based on my own personal experience with imposter syndrome, as well as having coached hundreds of people, many of whom also have it, this definition could not be any more accurate.

While writing this book, I went to PublishYourPurpose.com to see what I may have previously written about imposter syndrome and found the phrase often referenced in our interviews on the *Invisible Stories: Write to Be Seen* podcast.[16] You can listen to nearly any episode we've aired and hear the conversation pivot toward feeling like an imposter at some point or another. I don't think any of us are immune to this feeling during the process of writing a book. Writing a book is a huge deal. If you have doubts creeping in throughout this process, please know you're not alone, and you *can* move through this.

The book you're reading now is the seventh book I've written, and I've felt like an imposter more times than I can count in my many years of writing. Even as I'm typing these words, the question, *What will the editors think of my writing?* has crossed my mind a dozen times.

---

15 "Imposter Syndrome," Psychology Today, accessed March 7, 2023, https://www.psychologytoday.com/us/basics/imposter-syndrome.
16 https://publishyourpurpose.com/podcast/

> When we're able to see clearly what our vision is in a three-dimensional way, it brings us that much closer to making our book-writing dream a reality.

Imposter syndrome shows up in our lives all the time. We often feel it in moments when we're doing something scary or out of our comfort zones and our brains want to knock us down a few pegs as a way to protect us, specifically our egos. Asking the question, "What if no one buys this book?" is a common sign of imposter syndrome because we can easily rationalize by answering, "Oh, no one will" and then stop working on it. It's a form of self-sabotage that can really get the best of us if we aren't fully prepared for it.

You don't need to be the expert on all things related to your topic to write the book and be an author. You don't. It's a myth that we have to be the absolute, foremost subject-matter expert on the topic. Your unique angle is more than enough. Your experience is more than enough. *You are enough.* Reread this again if you're still struggling: You. Are. Enough.

Commit to Yourself

I encourage you to visit www.PublishYourPurpose.com/book-extras to download the printable "Commitment to Myself" document. This is a very simple document, but what it does is put the commitment of writing your book in front of you in an intentional way. Hang it on your fridge, put it in your car—anywhere that you'll see it on a regular basis. When you have that moment of doubt and start to question your motives, you can see that you made this commitment to yourself and that is what matters most.

Elizabeth Marvel's quote, "If you can see it, you can be it"[17] absolutely applies here. If you can see your vision of being a published author, then having a constant reminder of that belief and goal can really help you on this journey. This is also why we began with knowing your purpose, your vision, your impact, and your goals. With this added insight, you're able to lean into your uniqueness and into why you're the best person to write your book.

---

17 Debra Birnbaum, "'Homeland' Star Elizabeth Marvel: 'It's a Wonderful Time' to Be Playing the President-Elect," *Variety*, January 13, 2017, https://variety.com/2017/tv/news/homeland-star-elizabeth-marvel-its-a-wonderful-time-to-be-playing-the-president-elect-1201960319/.

If you hit a block in your writing because that imposter is screaming in your head, get up and switch tasks. Take your dog for a walk, listen to a podcast, call a friend, or do a work-related task—something to get you out of the manuscript for a little bit to recharge. I find doing something physically active is what works best for me. If I'm feeling blocked or sense the imposter is coming in a little too hot at that moment, I'll get up and move my body so that I can physically move that negative energy through, and out of, my system.

Author Fatigue

Not only does the imposter in us wreak havoc on our mindset, but it can also sometimes cause us to feel fatigued or burned out. Writing a book can be a long and emotional process that can take months or even years to finish, depending on how much time you dedicate to it. When you're in the thick of it, you may start to feel overwhelmed about the number of pages you have left to write, feel stuck on a section you're currently writing, or feel down about your abilities. All of these are signs of author fatigue.

Author fatigue is when you're mentally struggling with your writing and feel tired or overwhelmed about it. It's a literal exhaustion from writing that leads to burnout and why many people who start writing a book don't finish. You may lose motivation through the writing process or struggle to write about the concepts that you had laid out in your outline. The mental block and writer's block can persist for days or weeks, leaving you frustrated and questioning why you decided to write a book in the first place.

It's completely normal to struggle with author fatigue at any point during the writing process, and it can take shape in a number of ways. Questioning the purpose of writing your book, experiencing fear that your audience will never even read your work, and lack of motivation to write for days at a time are also signs of author fatigue.

Author fatigue builds on itself. Worrying day in and day out about how your writing will turn out can lead to you not wanting to write at all. The important thing is to recognize the signs and take time for yourself to recover and push through it. Fortunately, there are a few ways to push through this author fatigue to get you back on track!

> If you can see your vision of being a published author, then having a constant reminder of that belief and goal can really help you on this journey.

Take a Mental Health Day

If you're following a writing schedule, take a day off. Give yourself permission to take time for yourself. Use the time that you would've spent writing to do something relaxing or something that relaxes you. This can be taking a walk in a park, meditating, enjoying a relaxing bath, or spending time with friends or family—whatever you need to do to take your mind away from your writing so that when you come back to it, you're able to write with a clear head.

Take a Step Back from Your Writing

There may be times when you need more than a day to get reenergized and back into a writing routine. If you start to notice that you're really struggling with your writing and overthinking how everything will come together, allow yourself to put down your manuscript for a week. Take time for yourself and do other tasks that you need to focus on, take a mini vacation, do what you feel is right and what will reenergize you, and let your thoughts on your manuscript sit in the back of your mind.

Also do things you've been putting off during this time because you've prioritized your writing and your book. You may come up with some good ideas and concepts that you jot down during a particular week that you want to remember when you go back to writing. When that week is up, you'll be refreshed and ready to continue where you left off. Though, you want to make sure that either you or someone else is holding you accountable (more on this in the next chapter) to the timeline that you've set. It's incredibly easy to completely fall off the wagon, which isn't the desired outcome.

Write about Other Things

Writing about other topics that don't revolve around your book's topic can give you a jolt of inspiration and help you continue to meet your writing goals. It can be exhausting to continually write about the same topic. Having a change of pace and writing about something else can help you push through those points and keep the creative juices flowing.

Even if you take time to write about other topics, you're still putting words on paper and engaging the creative process. You don't need to have some big topic to write about; you can write about your day, something that's been on your mind through journaling, or a creative piece. This will keep you in the rhythm of writing and will help you get through author fatigue.

Do Other Book-Related Things

If you're struggling to get words down on paper but want to keep making progress on your book, you can do things for your book that don't necessarily involve writing. These can be brainstorming or finding inspiration for your cover design, thinking about the title of your book, or buying small things for your book such as a display shelf. These are all contributing to your book even if you aren't focusing on the writing part. You're able to give yourself a break from your writing and prioritize other parts of your book so that you're still working on the finished product, all the while making sure you don't get fatigued from writing. And doing these book-related but non-writing things may also provide inspiration to return to the writing aspect of your book.

Bottom Line: You Can Do This!

At the end of the day, your mindset can either be your life raft or a lighthouse, depending on what you need at the time. The trick is sticking to your goal of getting your book written while being mindful and intentional about what your mind, heart, and body need during this process. The more in tune you are, the better your chances of success.

GROW FURTHER

Join the Publish Your Purpose Author Lab workshop to take your learning experience offline and into a supportive online group environment where you can work on your mindset in a safe space.

Access the workshop here:
https://publishyourpurpose.com/author-lab/.

PROMOTE YOUR PURPOSE

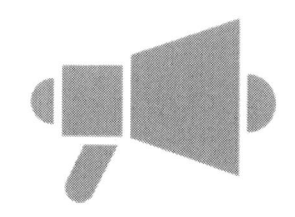

Start Calling Yourself an Author

All writers are not authors and not all authors consider themselves writers. Calling yourself an author is a state of mind, and it can feel confronting when you haven't written your manuscript or haven't even written one word yet. That's okay—this is a journey. Start calling yourself an author today. It will help you gain the confidence you'll need when your book is published and the concrete marketing begins.

CHAPTER 4
Accountability and Support Systems

Working on your book can be an isolating process and, often, a stressful experience. We're often alone and in our thoughts for endless hours. For some of us, being alone in our thoughts is a wonderful place to be, filled with excitement and exploration. For others, this is a terrifying experience.

When we think about the writing process, we don't often think about how we're going to handle and manage the emotional side when it inevitably arises. We'll get into best practices for your writing in Part 2, but before we get there, let's talk about how we can set you up for the best success.

Support Systems

Having the right support system can make or break your book writing and publishing experience. Surrounding yourself with those who believe in you and have your best interest in mind can be a determining factor in whether you complete the task of writing your book. We have enough inner critics living within our minds that we need to minimize the critics who exist in the flesh.

In my personal experience of having written seven books, as well as having coached hundreds of people, I've learned that there are three types of people you want to have on your side in this process: a Strategist, a Therapist, and a Cheerleader.

One person can fill multiple roles, or different people can fulfill different roles for you. You won't need all three of these simultaneously all the time, but you *will* need each of these at some point while you're writing your book. These people don't necessarily need to be professionals that you pay; they can be friends or family who are in your corner while you're writing your book. Let's dive into a bit more detail about each of these roles.

The Strategist

This is the most important of the three people you'll need. The Strategist is the person who looks at everything from a 30,000-foot view. This can be a project manager, a writing coach, a publishing coach, or a mentor. You'll need to have someone who can look at the bigger picture from start to finish and help you stick to a timeline for publishing your book. While you're writing your book, they will strategize what the plan is after you finish writing.

Your Strategist will also be the one who will keep you on track throughout your writing and publishing timelines. They'll help oversee your progress, make sure you're sticking to the subject you're writing about, and ensure you don't get overwhelmed by the number of tasks that need to be completed today or in the future.

While you need to be thinking about the wider scope of the publishing process from day one, it can be overwhelming to think about all the tasks that need to be accomplished. This is where your Strategist will lay out a concrete plan for you to follow. Whether that plan is on a daily, weekly, or monthly basis is up to you and how you best operate. A good Strategist will work with you and what you feel most comfortable with so that you don't get overwhelmed and driven to the point where you feel it's impossible to publish your book.

Your Strategist will also help create a marketing plan from day one and ensure that your book gets off the ground and into the hands of your readers. They'll help you figure out where your audience is and the best way to reach them and will answer questions such as how your book will fit into your business and how you can leverage your book to elevate your business. Working with you, they'll come up with a book launch and post-publication plan. The last thing you want is to publish your book and then have boxes of them stored in your house, used as paperweights because you had no distribution strategy.

This may be the hardest person to identify within your existing network. You'll want somebody who has a shared vision for you and the wherewithal to be your North Star to ensure you're aligned with your purpose, vision, impact, and goals. But if you look, you'll find them—and hey, it just might be someone at PYP.

The Therapist

Your Therapist can be an actual therapist or a friend, life coach, or business coach who will help you through the process emotionally. Writing about your personal experiences can bring about unexpected emotions that can take a toll on you. You may be writing about something from your past or something that's traumatic, and once it's on paper it will start to feel like Pandora's box. When you're writing about personal experiences that are near and dear to your heart, it can feel like you're reliving those experiences all over again. Having someone you can vent to or confide in will help you through these experiences when you're writing.

In dire times, your Therapist will be the one who will pull you off the metaphorical ledge and help you get back on track. The stress of publishing may overwhelm you to the point of feeling like you can't write or finish your book. Your Therapist is the one who will talk you through those moments and help get you back on your feet.

When I'm working with authors, there are days when I'm intentionally putting them on that ledge and days when I'm talking them off it. There must be a good balance of extending beyond your comfort zone. Your words can't be nearly as impactful if you write from just where you're most comfortable. It's the tension and dance both within and outside of your comfort zone that can really resonate with your readers.

The Therapist's job is to listen to you and help you work through the emotional things that come up that you may need to talk about. When you're writing about topics that pertain to your life or about past events, unexpected emotions may come up. Some of those emotions may arise from unresolved issues that have happened in your past and need to be unpacked with someone. Talking with a professional can help you get to the root cause of your emotions and resolve those feelings. They are also there to support you in your work and your writing. In the same vein as having a friend or a writing group offering advice, your Therapist can also offer their own input for your writing.

Going beyond writing, there's the large task of planning the rest of your book. Figuring out what the cover design will look like, making sure that you have the right editor, and creating and executing your marketing strategy are huge stressors. Your Therapist will listen to you vent and talk to you about the struggles you're facing during these steps. They need to be someone who's an active listener, encourages you, and gives you advice (when needed) about what to focus on next and the goals you have in front of you.

The Cheerleader

Your Cheerleader doesn't have to do splits and wave pom-poms in the air, but they will be someone who encourages you while you're writing your book. They will be the one who lifts you up while you're down. Writing a book is challenging and there *will* be low points, such as feeling bogged down by writing every day or every week or like you aren't making any progress because you skipped a writing session.

You may doubt and question yourself during the process, thinking things like *Why am I writing this book?* and *Who will even read my book?* Your Cheerleader will be the person who reminds you that you have a purpose in writing your book. As much as they cheer you on and support you while you're writing, they will also be there to help pick you back up when you've fallen down.

When you're bogged down with figuring out aspects of your book, your Cheerleader will help provide that positive encouragement that makes you feel like you can take on the world. That positive energy boost will help you make it through the lowest lows and elevate the highest highs. This person should be there not only when the going gets tough but also when you hit those high moments to boost your positivity and productivity further.

> Your words can't be nearly as impactful if you write from just where you're most comfortable.

Your Cheerleader can be your spouse or partner (if you have one) or a close friend, and in many cases the role can be filled by different people. If you have a spouse or partner that may not be as supportive or encouraging as you need them to be, that's okay. Someone else can be your Cheerleader—a writing group that you go to, for example, or maybe your best friend who has also written a book. Your Cheerleader is the person who can provide that support for you and encourage you to keep going.

The Magic Trio

I first began telling people that I was a Strategist, Therapist, and Cheerleader when working with authors. It started as a joke, but over time I and my team truly saw the power of having these three roles involved in both the writing and publishing processes.

As mentioned earlier, you don't need to have all three at the same time. Depending on how you work and process, you may not need a Strategist until you've written the first draft of your manuscript. You may not need a Therapist until you reach a certain part of your book where you encounter some unexpected emotion, and you may not need a Cheerleader until you're in the throes of marketing. When you need each person depends on you and how you're able to process these experiences.

However, it's important to have these three people at some point during the publishing process. Asking a friend or a group in advance, saying that you may need a Cheerleader or Therapist in the future, will ensure that they and you are prepared when you need them. This way, when the time comes and you need one, two, or all three of these people, you won't have to scramble trying to figure out who can fill what role for you.

It can be hard to anticipate where you may struggle or where you may need someone's shoulder to lean on, especially if you've never gone through this process before. When you'll need each person is entirely dependent on you, but having someone there through the highs and lows will make this all a bit easier.

At PYP, we know the emotional toll that writing a book can take on an author, so we intentionally fill all three of these roles whenever an author needs them. We commit ourselves to helping in any way necessary in order to get their book published and their story told.

Let's Talk About Who's On Your Team

REMINDER: *Visit www.PublishYourPurpose.com/book-extras to download the free workbook that goes with this book.*

Now that you know the three people you need in your support network, let's take a few minutes to fill in the blanks. I invite you to download the worksheet that will allow you to fill in who will play these roles in your life as an author.

STRATEGIST	THERAPIST	CHEERLEADER
1.	1.	1.
2.	2.	2.
3.	3.	3.
4.	4.	4.
5.	5.	5.

IF This, THEN That

Not only do we want names in those boxes, we want to go one step further and put a plan in place for when the unexpected occurs. This is the next phase of our support system—having a plan in place for when things go wrong. Life will get in the way; that's undeniable. What we do about it is what will make or break the success of our book project.

At PYP, we've found a simple way to prepare you for how to handle life when it comes rolling at you at an inconvenient time: the "if this, then that" statement. This statement is common in computer programming and can be a game changer in writing your book. And the good news is that it is very simple to create.

Think about an average day in your life. Who or what do you instinctively know will somehow get in your way at some point? Do you have long work hours and a lot of responsibility and know that someone on your team is going to need you at the exact wrong moment when you're working on your book? Do you have a family who doesn't have boundaries and will absolutely interrupt you regardless of the Do Not Disturb sign on your door? Do you know that there are areas in your book you need to write about and explore but that you've had trouble in the past getting them on paper?

Regardless of where you land in all of this, there's a simple way to set yourself up for success: spend a few minutes brainstorming all of the ways you can anticipate being thrown off your writing game and write them down.

It's Your Turn

Now, go ahead and brainstorm what you could do to turn around all the situations you just identified. What could you do differently that will give you the time or space to continue in your writing without interruption or distraction?

The next step is to put these situations into IF this, THEN that statements, which are quite simple. Here are two examples:

> *IF I am interrupted by my family,* **THEN** *I will schedule my writing time for when they are asleep OR I will leave the house to write.*
>
> *IF I am triggered by something in my past,* **THEN** *I will talk to a friend about it OR I will schedule time with my therapist.*

Do you see how simple and yet powerful having these statements can be? It gives us space to predict what we expect to distract us and to have a plan in place for what to do when that happens. This can be a game changer for getting us back on track when we inevitably fall off and into life's everyday pressures.

Use the space on the following page or download the worksheet to work through some of your own personal examples.

MY BACKUP PLAN (FILL IN THE BLANKS)

IF

THEN

IF

THEN

IF

THEN

IF

THEN

> If you're writing a book and you know you will accomplish this one way or another, the best thing to do is start telling people right now, at this very moment, that you're writing your book.

Accountability

If we think about anything in life, we can see that accountability plays an important role in getting things done. When it comes to writing, we're often doing it in a silo, with no external pressure or accountability. One of the most effective ways to ensure you cross the book-writing finish line is by introducing external accountability to your writing process.

When it comes to marketing your book, it's a myth that you should start this process after you've written it or, dare I say, after you've published it. The marketing element of your book should be a focus even before you have the first word written on paper. This may sound counterintuitive or even disingenuous in some way.

If you're writing a book and you know you will accomplish this one way or another, the best thing to do is start telling people right now, at this very moment, that you're writing your book. That will give you instant accountability because you've now made a public declaration that your book is coming.

In working with many authors, I've noticed that this is where imposter syndrome often rears its ugly head. We start to say to ourselves, *How could I promote a book I haven't written yet?* and *What if I don't finish this and I've told everyone, will they think I'm a liar?* We then begin to unravel and spiral. When we set external pressure for ourselves, we need to come up with a plan that ensures we cross the finish line and don't become that feared liar.

Telling people you're writing a book looks different for everyone. You may want to go to your favorite social media channel and announce it to a specific group of followers, or you may want to broadcast it to everyone you know. You may want to consider including it in your next newsletter, or you may want to privately reach out to a small handful of people you trust and tell them. The more people you tell, the further you increase your chances of following through. But if you don't have any of these outlets, telling a small group of people will be just enough. You have to pick what feels right for you and remember that this is your journey to being a published author. It does not have to mirror that of the person sitting next to you.

For a little added fun, I encourage you, if you post on social media, to tag me or PYP in your posts. You can say something like, "I'm reading *Publish Your Purpose* by @jenntgrace at @publishyourpurpose and she's strongly urging me (read: forcing me) to post here to tell you that I'm writing a book. I'm nervous about it, but I know if I tell you I have a better chance of finishing this book."

The Power of a Completion Date

Yes, accountability and marketing go hand-in-hand. This is true, and I've seen this play out many times over. But what you really need to do to ensure you aren't a liar is set a completion date.

Setting a completion date is simple, and there are two ways to think about this. You can decide when you want to have your first draft written, or you can decide when you want to have your book published and in the hands of your readers. Which path you choose is entirely up to you. For reference, the publishing process usually takes about six months. At PYP, our publishing timeline is about six months, and I've found that many other publishers operate similarly. For the sake of easy numbers and math, if you know you want to have your book published and in the hands of your readers one year from today, allocate six months for publishing, and then you'll know that you have six months, starting now, to write your manuscript.

The next step will be to identify how much writing you need to do in those six months in order to create a manuscript that serves the purpose you're aiming for. In Part 2 we'll go into deep detail on exactly how to figure this out.

Accountability Partners

If you decide you want to have your book published one year from today, I encourage you to take that to your people—tell them. It's a big goal, it's a scary goal, but it's absolutely attainable. Getting the encouragement and support of your friends, family, colleagues, and clients will offset the amount of fear you might be experiencing.

You can take this a layer deeper and provide a routine update to those you've told. Whether you post to social media or text a friend, the benefits will be the same. You'll know that there's some sort of external accountability whether they are directly asking you or lurking in the distance. This can look like a simple message that says, "I worked on my manuscript this week" or a more specific one that says, "I wrote 1,000 words in my manuscript this week."

Accountability partners are part of your support system. Since writing and publishing a book can be an emotional rollercoaster, having an accountability partner to support you can make all the difference in you crossing the finish line.

The ideal scenario is having a partner who is also striving toward a big goal. If they are also writing a book, I believe that synergy will be stronger; but it could be a friend who's training for a marathon or some other big endeavor. The accountability will then be mutual. You'll be checking in with each other to ensure you're both moving forward with your goals.

Setting up a schedule or routine with your accountability partner is also critical. Instead of checking in with one another when either of you happens to remember, get in the habit of doing it at certain intervals. It could be that you send each other a text every morning. It could be that you pick one day per week when you'll check in via phone. Whatever works for you is how you should do this. The more thoughtful you are with how you want to approach this accountability, the greater your odds of it working will be.

What I've loved watching is that graduates of our *Getting Started for Authors* writing program[18] have paired up with one another to help each other see their writing through. While the goal of our writing program is to get a manuscript written in six months, sometimes that just doesn't happen for the aforementioned reasons. But the great thing is that, because there's a shared common goal, authors hold one another accountable so that they both cross the finish line of becoming an author.

---

18   https://publishyourpurpose.com/writing-support/

Bottom Line: You Can Do This!

There are so many simple ways to gather the right support system and right accountability structure to accomplish your goal of writing a book. You've already started the hard work of identifying your purpose, impact, vision, goals, mindset, and now accountability. In the next part of this book, we're going to dive into writing best practices so that you can maximize your efficiency in the writing process.

GROW
FURTHER

Join the Publish Your Purpose Author Lab workshop to take your learning experience offline and into a supportive online group environment where you can access a support system and additional accountability.

Access the workshop here:
https://publishyourpurpose.com/author-lab/.

PROMOTE YOUR PURPOSE

Update Your Email Signature

Many of us spend our days sending and receiving emails. Every email you send is an opportunity to speak to the fact that you're an upcoming author. Consider updating your email signature to include "Author" after your title. Or, if you know the title of your book already, consider adding "New Book Coming Soon: *Your Book Title Here.*"

This will be a conversation starter as people begin to see that you're working on a book. These same folks may be instrumental in the promotion of your book down the road. Start small, and stay in your inbox.

PART 2: WRITING

Welcome to Part 2: Writing. The following chapters are going to go into deep detail about everything you'll need to know to make the writing part of your book easier. We often think about how writing is such a creative process, but what we don't think about is that there's a science or formula to it as well. These chapters will break the writing process down in a way that will feel manageable and attainable so that you can get it done and begin to make an impact in the world.

CHAPTER 5
Your Target Reader

One of the most common mistakes when it comes to defining our target reader is that we wait until *after* the book is written to think about them. Target readers are important for both how the book is *written* and how the book is *sold*. If you wait until you finish your manuscript to think about who you're writing for or how you'll reach them, you'll unfortunately put yourself at a disadvantage.

The best way to approach the writing process is to understand who you're writing for before you put a single word on the page. This will ensure that your book is written for exactly who you're trying to reach. It can also influence things like what stories you share and what examples you use.

Who is Going to Read Your Book?

Let's dive into figuring out who you want to read your book. When you think of the phrasing of a target reader, you may have done something similar with a target market or target audience in your business. If you're writing a book that's closely aligned with your business, then you'll be ahead of the game because you'll have already identified who your target audience is and much of that information will cross over.

If you've never thought about a target anything, we'll start at the beginning. From a marketing standpoint, target markets are critical because they help us make decisions that will greatly impact our chances of success by ensuring the people we want to be in front of see us and resonate with what we have to say or offer.

Target markets/readers can be broken down into a few different buckets:

- Demographic
- Geographic
- Psychographic
- Behavioral

This chapter will go into detail on each of these buckets so that by the end of it you're able to write a book that resonates with the reader you're aiming to serve, thus making a bigger impact in their lives.

Exercise

REMINDER: *Visit www.PublishYourPurpose.com/book-extras to download the free workbook that goes with this book.*

I want you to spend a few minutes now and write down who you believe you're writing for, in as much detail as you can. Don't worry about what you don't know yet. Write down, as it stands, who your book is for. At the end of this chapter we're going to repeat this exercise, and you'll see how well you've been able to refine it as a result of what you've learned here.

What we're doing here is defining your target reader, which you may have heard people call an avatar or a target audience. An avatar is a common marketing term to describe who you're trying to reach to buy your goods or services.

If you're more of a visual or auditory learner, you're welcome to check out the target reader lesson from the Publish Your Purpose Author Lab workshop. This is a free multi-day workshop that PYP runs a couple of times a year. I encourage you to check out the most recent replays by going here: www.publishyourpurpose.com/author-lab.

Now that you've written down who your ideal target reader is, let's dive into the four pillars of target readers. I'll put the caveat here that as you go through these pillars, some will feel like they don't fit—that's okay. Not everything will be relevant to you and your book.

Demographic Data

Let's start with demographic data. I find that demographic data tends to be the easiest to understand and is the information most authors already know about their readers:

- How old are your readers?
- What type of occupation/job do they have?
- Where did they grow up?
- What is their educational background?
- What is their sexual orientation or gender identity?
- What is their race, ethnicity, or cultural background?
- What is their marital status?
- What generation are they from?

Think of demographic data as data that you can easily check a box for. This data is important because this will help you narrow down how to find those readers through your marketing outreach.

Geographic Data

Geographic data may or may not be relevant. If it doesn't feel like this fits, you can move on to the next pillar. Geographic data relates to data points relevant to where your readers live:

- Where do your potential readers live (either now or in the past)?
- In what country or region of the world?
- What language is spoken?
- What is the environmental climate like? Are there four seasons? Is it warm year-round?
- Do they live in an urban or suburban environment?

Remember, this may or may not be relevant to the book you're writing—and that's okay! You have permission to ignore these questions.

Psychographic Data

Psychographic data differs from demographic data in that it's about what makes people do the things they do rather than box-checking facts:

- What type of lifestyle do they lead and why?
- What type of environment do they live in?
- What was their background or upbringing?
- What type of responsibility do they have in the workplace?
- What news sources do they read or listen to?
- What social media channels do they prefer to be on?

Behavioral Data

Behavioral data is exactly what it sounds like; it's how people behave and what their preferences are. This information will be an incredible asset in your marketing efforts because it tells you how to reach your target reader.

Two questions we can bring directly from the psychographic data section are—

- What news sources do they read or listen to?
- What social media channels do they prefer to be on?

But other questions to think about are—

- What motivates your readers?
- Are they avoiding pain?
- Are they seeking pleasure?
- Are they someone who can be influenced?
- Are they the influencer?
- Are they an impulse shopper?
- Are they likely to belong to a book club or study group?
- What format of book do they consume? Print? Audio? Ebook?
- Do they prefer to loan books out at the library?

> We often forget that not everyone knows someone who has written a book, so you might be the first someone writing a book in your network or community.

Are you starting to see how this information can be incredibly valuable in determining how to reach your intended reader?

Psychographic data and behavioral data will certainly have some crossover. The beautiful part about doing this exercise is that it'll help you get into the mind of your target reader in a completely different way. This will have a direct impact on how to reach your target reader down the road because you'll have a better sense of what makes them tick.

If you find the questions, the worksheet, or even this chapter a little overwhelming, I encourage you to slow down and revisit it as often as you need to. This is an integral part of the process that is worth slowing down for because it will influence every other aspect of your writing journey. You can watch a video replay of our Publish Your Purpose Author Lab workshop by visiting PYP's website at www.publishyourpurpose.com/author-lab.

An important item to note here is that not all readers are buyers and not all buyers are readers. This is something to keep in mind as you think about how you're going to market to them. For example, you might be writing a book for entry-level employees of a company. A book like *Who Moved My Cheese* is a very popular book intended for new employees of a company. The first CEO I worked for had me read it when I was 23. As a 23-year-old I wasn't seeking that book out, but I was the intended reader of it. That book was not written for the CEO, but he was the buyer of the book. Do you see the point here?

Now is the time to pull apart the question of, *Is my reader also my buyer?* And if the answer is no, this is where you'll start a separate notes section where you can identify who your target market is for your book; not the reader, as they will be two separate entities. Your book will be written for your target *reader*, but it'll be marketed to the target *buyer*.

Finding More Information

Go back through the previous section and pull out the areas you feel most concerned about—the areas where you believe it might be difficult to find this information. Identify two or three questions and determine how you'll get insights and answers to them.

Your question might look like, *Where are my target readers getting book recommendations from?* Or you could be asking yourself, *If I wrote my story, who would be interested in reading it?* There's no need to guess when you can source data that can influence your approach. This isn't the time to make wild guesses in the dark; there are tangible ways to get this information, which include asking your clients, those on your mailing list, or those connected to you on social media.

I fully acknowledge the fear that may be coming up for you as you think about asking people you know for the answers to this information. What I know to be true, though, is that the more people who know you're writing a book, the more support you'll gain from those same people later in the process.

We often forget that not everyone knows someone who has written a book, so you might be the first someone writing a book in your network or community. As a result, people are going to be excited and want to come along with you for the ride. Engaging people at the very onset of the process by asking them questions about themselves, their habits, and their preferences will help you grow your audience of people who are going to be patiently waiting for your book to come out further down the road.

Blogging

You could write a blog entry, post it to your website, and give people the option to comment on it. Ask them specific questions that you're hoping to get answers to and see what happens. Ask things like, "Do you like the usage of the phrase 'Grow Your Big Idea' in the subtitle?" You could choose to write them in an open-ended way or a very simple yes or no structure. There are pros and cons to each. With open-ended questions, you often get much more information and insight by allowing people to answer based on where their minds specifically go. You could rephrase to, "What do you think of when you see the phrase 'Grow Your Big Idea' in the subtitle?" But with a simple yes or no, it might be easier for people to complete because they're just checking a box and don't have to think. The benefit of this is you might end up with more data, but it may not be data that will really help inform your next steps or get to the bottom of what you're determined to find out.

Social Media

You can also bring your questions to social media. We know that there is no shortage of opinions on social media, so just remember to take feedback with a grain of salt. Readers of your blog and subscribers to your mailing list have a stronger connection to you than someone on your social media who just happened to see your question and then wrote something inappropriate or unhelpful. Just remember that when you're deciding what information to incorporate in your plans, not all feedback is created equal.

Other Books

A really great way to get an understanding of who might be interested in your book is by doing competitive research on books comparable to yours. Follow those authors on social media, see what their engagement is with their readers, and pay attention to the comments. Are there any insights you can glean from this?

Is this author a *Forbes* contributor? Yes? Great! Go check out the comments section of their writing. Try to investigate where that author is seeing success. A little bit of internet stalking will go a long way. (And don't try to tell me you've never internet stalked someone—we all have.)

I find there's a gold mine of information within the Amazon and Goodreads reviews. If you spend any time in the reviews section of either of these sites, you'll find really valuable information. This will not only help you further refine your target reader but will help you frame your big-picture messaging for your book. If you sort the comments by top comments, you'll see where the author is really resonating with readers. Whether it's their tone, their ability to synthesize information in a way that's easy to understand, or the brilliant way their content was laid out—this is all really good information for you. It's the information that you can consider using as you approach the structure of your book (more on that in Part 2).

In reverse, what you'll want to do is filter by the worst comments, the most critical, and the harshest. This will give you insights into where the author missed the mark—and to me, this is where your real opportunity lies. If you can see where that author failed, it's your opportunity to shine and *not* follow in their footsteps.

The purpose of all of this is to shorten your process by being more clear about who you're writing for, how you'll reach them with your message, and how you'll do it better than the author who launched their book before you. You can approach the same topic, the same genre, the same concept, but in a different way—one that will resonate with your readers in the way that you want it to resonate with them.

Use Google

A final strategy to think about here is Googling your readers' demographics. If you're writing a book about caregivers, you may want to simply type in something like "family caregiver demographics." This will bring you search results that are somehow tied (ideally) to what you're looking for. In this search, you might find that there's a robust website, association, magazine, or publication that focuses on family caregivers, and you can begin to read their information and see what direction this takes you in.

If you come across a publication or association, for example, there's a strong possibility that you'll find information about advertising or sponsorships. That's where you may find hard, concrete data that's in direct alignment with who you're writing your book for. They'll have done the homework and research on who their audience is, which may mirror and match your ideal reader very closely.

From a future marketing standpoint, you may want to start developing relationships with these organizations and publications because your book will align with the needs of their audience, which could open up a lot of marketing possibilities for you. This could include being a guest columnist for them where you teach their audience something and can then subtly promote your book at the end of each article. Or you may be invited to be a virtual guest teacher for their audience. These are incredible audience-building activities that will help your book land in the hands of your ideal reader in a seamless way.

Your Writing Style

Let's look at your writing style, which may not really fit any of the aforementioned buckets neatly but rather crosses all of them in one way or another.

There are many different ways you can approach your writing style, but I find that there are two primary ways: academic and casual. Within academic and casual writing are many subsets, but these are overarching ways to think about it.

If you're writing a book for the average person, writing in an academic style is going to be a disadvantage to your reader. If you're writing a book for an academic audience, writing in a more casual and relaxed style isn't going to gain you the respect that you deserve in your field.

You may have heard in the past that you should write for a seventh-grade-level reading comprehension.[19] This still remains true. If your goal is to write a book that's accessible to your readers, you'll want to ensure that you're using language they understand and resonates with them. You don't want to make assumptions about diction such as, *Of course everyone knows that word,* because chances are, they may not.

Accessibility within books is really important because you never want your readers to feel less than others. You want them to read your book and walk away feeling empowered. Often, writers and authors feel they have to prove their worth to their readers by using big vocabulary or writing in a complex way. But what readers really want is to like you and feel you're relatable.

So the first thing you'll want to do is see where you fall in your writing style. If you're writing a how-to book or teaching your readers how to implement some kind of change in their lives, do yourself and them a favor and write in an accessible way. If you're writing for an academic audience, you'll want to make sure your writing style matches the standards set forth in the academic community. This book has been written for folks in the former group, those looking to write accessibly in order to create the biggest impact possible.

---

[19] George R. Klare, *The Measurement of Readability* (Ames, IA: University of Iowa Press, 1963).

Once you've determined where you land in the style of writing you'll take, you'll want to think a bit further about how you naturally write. Are you a naturally wordy writer? Are you a naturally conversational writer? Are you naturally an academic writer? Ideally, wherever you naturally fall is the direction you should head in.

For example, you'll see (or it's my hope that you see) that this book you're reading is written in a very conversational way. Making information accessible to authors is a core focus at PYP. While I hold advanced degrees and could've written incredibly complicated and verbose material to prove my worth to you, I didn't. I want everyone to understand the content of this book, and I've learned that my natural writing style is conversational, so when I'm writing my goal is to double down on that natural nature.

Bottom Line: You Can Do This!

As I said at the start of this chapter, this is going to be a lot of information. You have access to the companion workbook to utilize and take advantage of by putting all of your inspired thoughts down on paper. This is probably the heaviest chapter of this entire book because it's the most detailed and will have an enormous impact on the success of your book. I urge you to not take this chapter lightly and to revisit it as much as you need. This is an ongoing process that you won't perfect from the start—and that's okay.

I'd like you to revisit the exercise you did at the start of this chapter and do it again. Now that you have this new approach and new information, go through those same questions again and see if you have more clarity on who it is that you're writing for. If you aren't 100 percent there yet, that's okay; this will continue to be an evolution.

Simply being intentional about who you're writing for while you're writing will put you ahead of many other authors. Take your time and stay the course. You can do this!

GROW FURTHER

Join the Publish Your Purpose 30-Day Book Writing Challenge to create momentum, access accountability, and get one step closer to a rough first draft by having 30 days of writing tips delivered to your inbox daily.

Access the challenge here:
https://publishyourpurpose.com/30-day-book-writing-challenge/.

PROMOTE YOUR PURPOSE

Make a List of Buyers

Take a few minutes to make a list of people who you believe will buy your book. This isn't a fantasy list of who you desire to buy your book, but rather a practical list of people in your life and professional networks that you believe you can count on to buy your book when it becomes available.

This list will become increasingly more important as people directly tell you that they want you to notify them when your book is available. This list will ensure that you don't lose track of who is interested.

CHAPTER 6
How Long Should Your Book Be?

This chapter is going to add math into our writing equation—fear not, it's not that scary. I'm logical and pragmatic, yet math isn't my jam. But I've used this process to write all seven of my books, and it's the process we teach our authors in both our free Publish Your Purpose Author Lab workshop[20] and our Getting Started for Authors writing program.[21] I'm telling you, it was a game changer for me when I discovered this formula and I've been hooked ever since. We've now entered the writing section of this book, so we're about to create an easy-to-follow plan!

How Many Pages or How Many Words?

What I find first-time authors do *not* pay attention to is how long their book is or how long they desire their book to be. I'll often ask the question, "How many words are in your draft manuscript?" and they'll answer with, "About 90 pages." The publishing industry operates around word count, so it's a common question for service providers to ask you—from editors to typesetters to cover designers, it's a question most need an answer to. The challenge with using a page count versus a word count is that there are many variables with page count, such as the font size you're using, the width of the margins in your document, and how many headings or subheadings you might have. Your 90 pages may be 10,000 words and my

---
20   https://publishyourpurpose.com/author-lab
21   https://publishyourpurpose.com/writing-support/

90 pages may be 50,000 words. This makes it difficult to understand what the publishing costs may be (more on this in Part 3).

Now that you see that quantifying your book based on the number of pages isn't going to serve you well, let's talk about how many words you should aim for. Once upon a time, bigger was better in the world of books. The fact that authors from centuries past typically got paid for quantity over quality is how we landed in this world of large, voluminous books. In today's reading climate, bigger may actually hurt your chances of getting published and/or your success in sales.

It's never been a better time to be a non-fiction writer. Self-improvement book sales are at an all-time high,[22] and memoirs are on the rise.[23] Introspection is trendier than ever, and with the world finally waking up to the importance of having diverse stories and perspectives, you no longer have to be famous to publish—you just need an interesting story or angle.

Here's Why Size Matters

Having one big "megabook" is a thing of the past. When it comes to non-fiction, concision is key. Readers have developed an appreciation for specialists who dive deep into a topic rather than scratch the surface of multiple topics. Your goal is to understand your target audience's question or issue, and then resolve that question or issue as succinctly and directly as possible. Here are some reasons you're better off keeping it short.

> **Short Sells**
>
> How many pages is a good book? Let's look at sales trends. The average length of the *New York Times* bestseller decreased by 11.8 percent from 2011 to 2021.[24] While in the first half of the 2010s, books with 400+ pages (approximately 80,000–90,000 words)

---

22   Jim Milliot, "Self-Improvement Boom Sets Book Sales Off on Fast Start in 2021," Publishers Weekly, January 14, 2021, https://www.publishersweekly.com/pw/by-topic/industry-news/bookselling/article/85316-book-sales-get-off-to-fast-start.html.

23   Emily Donaldson, "What the Rise of the Memoir Has Meant for Non-Fiction," The Globe and Mail, September 17, 2021, https://www.theglobeandmail.com/arts/books/article-you-must-remember-this-the-rise-and-rise-of-memoir/.

24   Dimitrije Curcic, "Bestselling Books Have Never Been Shorter," WordsRated, June 20, 2022, https://wordsrated.com/bestselling-books-have-never-been-shorter/.

stayed on the bestseller list 4.4 weeks longer than their counterparts, this trend reversed in the second half of the decade, as books with less than 400 pages stayed on the list for 1.9 weeks longer between 2016 and 2021.

- **Short Attention Spans**
  Attention spans are shorter than ever. Readers lose interest if they catch you repeating yourself. A shorter book means you've synthesized your thoughts in the most efficient way possible.

- **Reader Engagement Is Essential**
  If you want your book to work for you, you need to be intentional about how you want the reader to engage with you *beyond* the book. A good book will have strong calls to action for reader engagement, which is a huge part of your marketing and business strategy.

Let's Do The Math

The length of your book will depend on whether you're writing a non-fiction book (i.e., you're teaching something) or a memoir (i.e., you're sharing your story in the hopes to teach or inspire your readers).

As a general rule of thumb, non-fiction books are best between 100 and 250 pages (20,000–60,000 words) and should rarely be more than 250 to 300 pages (of course there are always exceptions depending on your target audience). Memoirs can be longer, between 240 and 520 pages (60,000–130,000 words).

Knowing that a non-fiction book is best between 20,000 and 60,000 words, here's where we can break this down into manageable chunks for you to work with. Rather than staring at a blank screen and blinking cursor with the panic of knowing you need to write a book, we can break this down in a way that will feel easier to accomplish. Writing a book without a plan may feel like you're trying to boil the ocean. Let's start with boiling one cup of water at a time.

If you haven't already downloaded the accompanying workbook, now is the time to do so at www.PublishYourPurpose.com/book-extras. The following steps are best approached with a cheat sheet. There's also a video replay from the most recent Publish Your Purpose Author Lab workshop that will help you walk through this process if you're a more auditory or visual learner.[25]

STEP 1: Decide How Many Words You Want Your Book to Be

Decide how many words you want your book to be. A range of 20,000–60,000 is pretty wide and allows for flexibility. You want to be mindful of what length of book your readers are interested in reading. Start by looking at books similar to what you're up to. If you see that the majority of books in your genre are 200+ pages, it may appear that that is the going length for your target reader. But if we go back to an earlier tip—read the reviews on Amazon or Goodreads and see what people are saying about that particular book. You may see that readers are upset because the author was repetitive or that it just felt too long. That might be an opportunity for you to come in with something that's smaller and more succinct, and that will satisfy your readers.

Also, think about your readers' mindset. This is why Chapter 5, about the target reader, is so important. I'll give you an example from a book we published at PYP.

CASE STUDY

We had an author who was writing about hoarding and chronic disorganization. As she was writing her book, she knew that if she wanted to reach someone who is struggling with chronic disorganization, a long book was likely not the way to go. Instead, she packaged and presented her materials in a way that kept the information easy and succinct so that the reader could pick it up, gain insight, and put it down without being overwhelmed. The result was a 20,000-word book that was approximately 100 pages—because this is what her reader needed. If she had written a 60,000-word, 250-page book, there's a strong likelihood

---

25 https://publishyourpurpose.com/author-lab

that this would have been incredibly overwhelming for someone who is already experiencing chronic disorganization. This is why we must know our readers as intimately as we can. It gives us information that helps us make better decisions that impact the entire writing and publishing process—and most importantly the reader experience.

For the sake of following along, select a word count you feel suits what you're up to best. Please note, this is *not* set in stone. This is just a guidepost to help you craft a writing plan that will support you in getting your draft completed. Follow along with this example:

My goal is to write a 30,000-word book.

STEP 2: Determine Your Timeline

Determine a timeline. How quickly are you trying to get this book written? Do you have a concrete deadline? Do you have a big event that you want to have your book completed by so you can sell it to your ideal clients? This is the best place to start. I've worked with people who run the entire gamut of this. We once had an author who presold 2,500 copies of their book to a corporation before we even had a signed contract in place—talk about motivating!

Depending on your publishing path (more on this in Chapter 14), you'll want to allocate at least six months for the publishing process. If your dream is to have your book out one year from today, you have roughly six months to get your book written. If you want your book out in nine months, then you'll really have about three months to get your book written.

Alternatively, you may not have a set time frame in mind, as there's nothing urgently forcing you along. What I've found is that six months makes the perfect writing time frame. It gives you enough time that you don't have to rush, but it gives you a short enough time that you're able to keep your momentum going.

Again, for the sake of following along, pick a target time frame that feels reasonable to you or follow along with this example:

My goal is to write this book in six months.

> We must know our readers as intimately as we can. It gives us information that helps us make better decisions that impact the entire writing and publishing process—and most importantly the reader experience.

STEP 3: Figure Out How Much You Can Write

Our next step is to determine how many words you're able to write in a single writing session. A writing session, by my definition, is any period of time that you're dedicating to sitting down and getting your manuscript written. Here's where the math really starts to come in.

> **I want you to stop reading this book and do the following exercise. It will be critical in relation to the rest of this chapter and creating a concrete plan.**

Open Word, Google Docs, or Pages and set a timer for 30 minutes. I want you to write in that document until the timer goes off. Don't think too much about *what* you're writing about, just write. You could write about

- your book idea,
- why you're writing this book, or
- how your day went.

For the sake of this exercise, what you're writing isn't as relevant as it will be in the future. Once you complete this exercise, come back to the book. And again, if you haven't already downloaded the accompanying workbook, go get it here: www.PublishYourPurpose.com/book-extras. It's a lot easier when you have a place to write these numbers down.

Tick tock, tick tock.

Great, you're back! How many words were you able to write in that 30 minutes? Was it 200 words, 500 words, or 1,000 words? Whatever your number is, great! Please know this isn't a comparison with anyone else—this is about you and what works for you. Follow along with this example:

I was able to write 500 words in 30 minutes.

Now, your next step is to double that word count. If you were able to write 500 words in 30 minutes, we can safely assume that you can write 1,000 words per hour. Write this number down in your workbook.

I am able to write 1,000 words in one hour.

STEP 4: Set Your Writing Schedule

Let's find a writing schedule that works for you! Have you thought through how often you'd like to work on this book? Writing a book can be time-consuming, and without a plan it can feel endless. The beauty of what we're doing here is that we're setting parameters with real goals and metrics that you can work with. Take a look at the fullness of your life right now and determine how often you believe you can write in a week. It might be that, at the start, you can only carve out one hour per week to get your writing done. Or perhaps this is a top priority for you and, if that's the case, maybe you're able to write one hour per day for four days a week. Write this number down in your workbook.

> *I can commit to writing for one hour per week.*

Step 5: Put the Numbers Together

Let's look at how these numbers play out.

- *My goal is to write a 30,000-word book.*
- *My goal is to write this book in six months.*
- *I am able to write 1,000 words in one hour.*
- *I can commit to writing for one hour per week.*

If we follow along with my example, here's what we're able to see:

> 30,000 words / six months = five one-hour writing sessions per month = a little over one hour per week for the next six months

These five hours of writing per month might mean that you write for a little over one hour per week, or you may write for five days straight, one week per month. How you structure this is entirely up to you. Play with these numbers and see what starts to feel good.

Bottom Line: You Can Do This!

Can you see how much easier and less overwhelming writing your book can be when you have solid data to work with? Rather than staring at that blank screen thinking, *OMG, how am I going to write an entire book?* you can see that writing a book of your desired length may only take five hours per month over six months. This is a much better way to accomplish the big goal of writing your book and becoming a published author.

GROW FURTHER

Join the Publish Your Purpose 30-Day Book Writing Challenge to create momentum, access accountability, and get one step closer to a rough first draft by having 30 days of writing tips delivered to your inbox daily.

Access the challenge here:
https://publishyourpurpose.com/30-day-book-writing-challenge/.

PROMOTE YOUR PURPOSE

Make a List of Influencers

Building on your already created list of buyers, start a new column for people you know who have influence. The definition of an influencer here is anyone who has influence over a group of people. This could be a small book club of 10 people or a TikTok following of two million.

Most people don't have a social media influencer at their disposal for their book marketing, so think smaller. Who do you know that has influence over others? A board member of an organization that's relevant to you and your book? A friend who runs an online support group related to your topic? Whoever they are, write their name down. You'll want to use this in your book promotion later.

CHAPTER 7
Before You Begin Writing

By now I'm certain you're itching to begin writing your book with the new information you have. However, we have a little more information to get through for you to be truly set up for success. Having a strong plan and sense of direction with your book will save you a lot of time and headaches, so starting slow to go fast is the most efficient way to go.

This chapter is going to provide a resource that will continue to build on your previously established plan. And yes—we're going to bust out our math skills once again!

Ice Sculptures

Let's start off with an analogy (don't ask me about metaphors, though, as I'm the queen of mixing them up—for example, "The greasy bird gets the wheel.")

Stop for a moment and think about the last event you attended that had an ice sculpture. Was it at a wedding? A work event? Somewhere else? For me, it was at the Mystic Aquarium in Connecticut, where my son and I watched a man use a chainsaw to carve an ice sculpture of a sea lion. It was incredibly impressive!

When I think of ice sculptures, the first kind I think of are koi fish, the kind that point vertically with water flowing up through the fish and out its mouth. They are incredible works of art when you really slow down to see their beauty. What I want *you* to think about are the steps the artist took to get that sculpture to the place where it's impressive to onlookers. Did the artist just start carving it without a plan? Did they spend painstaking detail on one fin but not the other? And where did they get their block of ice from?

I'm sure these are questions you've never considered before because, honestly, why would you have needed to? Well, I'm here to show you how writing your book and carving an ice sculpture have a lot in common.

Let's start with the ice. Before there was a block of ice, there was water that had to be frozen. But even before the water was frozen, there had to be a container to put that water into. Your book is the same way. You can't just start carving (writing) without a container (outline).

We often want to hit the ground running and just start writing before we know what direction we're headed in. This is why having an outline is a critical component of this process. When we have an outline, we have a place to put our writing. Writing isn't a linear process, even though the reading process is. You don't need to start writing at the beginning and write chronologically or sequentially all the way to the end. You can write where you're inspired and, with an outline, you'll be able to drop your content into its respective location without stress or headaches.

Once the container (outline) has been established, we need to put water into it. The water is our disconnected and disorganized content. We really want to get whatever content that may have already existed into the container, so it can at least be accounted for (frozen).

Repurposing Content

One of the best time savers in writing your book is repurposing existing content. If you've been producing thought leadership of any kind, you're likely sitting on a treasure trove of previously created content that you may have never thought about reusing again. Why reinvent the wheel if you've already explained something really well somewhere else that you want to include in your book?

For example, perhaps you have a thought leadership paper in your business that's been a lead magnet for years and consistently helps bring in new clients. You may have invested in someone to help you edit it, design it, and then set it up on your website. That piece of content has proven to you that it's valuable and it works—why wouldn't you want to include that in your book, especially if a lot of the hard work is done already?

Chapter 15 of this book, "What to Ask a Publisher," is an example of exactly this. That chapter was designed from a PDF download that I give away to aspiring authors on a regular basis. It took a team of really talented people to put that content together, edit it, and design it. What did I do? Repurposed and modified it for your benefit in this book. You can see what this looks like here: www.publishyourpurpose.com/questions-ask-publisher.

You may also have a series of blog posts on your website that your clients and potential clients alike have commented on, about how much value they bring and how much they've helped them in solving their problem. Why not include that in your book?

This is the power of repurposing content. In addition to repurposing Chapter 14, there are other previously created blog posts, workshops, and webinar content that I've also scattered throughout this book. Again, you've spent a lot of time and effort doing it once, so there's absolutely nothing wrong with including it in your book. No one will hold your book in their hand and say, "How dare she include that blog post directly from her website?" If it provides value, it provides value, and no one is judging.

When you have a solid outline for where you want your book to go and where you want it to take your readers in their transformation, you can plug in your existing content and then see very clearly what content needs to be created next. That's the big opportunity—to see the content holes that are missing.

A Cautionary Tale

What I caution you about is being mindful of not taking everything you've written or created and putting it into one document because it will likely be overwhelming. Start with an outline, see what makes sense to bring in, and bring that information in specifically.

I made this mistake *big time* writing *this* book. You'd think after coaching hundreds of authors and writing seven books of my own that I would know better. I first began writing this book on July 9, 2020. I immediately brought in 165,428 words pulled from dozens of different places—blog posts, webinar transcripts, podcast interviews, you name it. Just a few months later, on September 17, 2020, I had 533,381 words in a single file. It was absolute madness that, in honesty, I'm still cleaning up.

With the average length of a book being about 50,000 words, having 11 times the amount of content I needed caused nothing but a headache, and at times it overwhelmed me. *Do not make this mistake.*

A Frozen Block of Ice

Once you assess what you've written toward your book and evaluate the existing content you may already have, you can see where the holes are and where you'll need to write new content. The next phase is freezing the water in the bucket. This is the real, true, shitty first draft.

Anne Lamott, author of the beloved book on writing, "Bird by Bird," coined the term "shitty first draft" in 1994. She emphasizes that the purpose of the first draft is simply to get your ideas onto the page, without judgment or self-editing. This process isn't pretty at all; it's an incomplete shitty first draft that still needs a lot of work. In other words, it's the water frozen in the bucket that the artist will begin carving the sculpture from. We want this to be in its shittiest and rawest form because this is where we'll begin to carve and turn it into the beautiful ice sculpture (finished book) that we know it can be.

Once you have that frozen block of ice, a.k.a. the shitty first draft, you can begin working your magic. An artist isn't going to spend all of their time carving the perfect head of a koi fish without paying any attention to the proportions of its body, so why would we do the same with our writing? The writing equivalent of this is making the first chapter absolutely perfect while giving no thought to the remaining chapters of the book or how it all connects together.

You want to think about your writing in passes. Start at the beginning and go through to the end. Make yourself notes, comments, and ideas of what you want to bring in and where. Then go through it again to refine it further, and again to refine that further, and so on and so forth—one pass at a time.

> Writing isn't a linear process, even though the reading process is.

What this will do is help you provide equal attention to all areas of the book. What we see at PYP over and over again is that the first half of the manuscript is in great shape, but the second half completely falls apart. I attribute this largely to writing in programs such as Word, Google Docs, or Pages. By default, when you open that document, you begin on Page 1 and scroll and scroll and scroll to get to where you last left off. What happens for many of us is that we open it on Page 1 and immediately begin to revisit Page 1, Chapter 1, rather than focusing on where we left off. This results in a disproportionate amount of time being spent in the earlier chapters of the book.

The Other Side of Your Shitty First Draft

On the other side of your shitty first draft will be your actual first draft, the first draft that you're feeling good about. The one that you'll continue to tweak and refine to get it to where you feel it's nearly ready to begin working on with an editor. In this case, imagine you can see the body of the koi fish. You can't really make out the fine details such as the lines in its tail, the spots on its body, or the shape of its eyes, but you can tell that it's a fish. That's where you want to be as you begin to enter the editing phase of this process. The editing phase is where all of that fine detail gets fleshed out and when your vision becomes a reality. We'll cover editing in Chapter 10.

Permission Granted

Writing a shitty first draft can bring up a lot of emotion. Imposter syndrome may creep in, leading you to believe that your work must be great immediately and that your first draft must be of really awesome quality. But the reality is that all books start off as shitty first drafts. It's the nature of this process, but sometimes we feel as if we need permission to write something shitty.

As a result, I hereby grant you permission to write your shitty first draft. Knowing what you know now, you can see that this is an iterative process. You don't write to perfection straight out of the gate—no one does, even the most well-known authors in the world.

Track Your Progress

The final area I want to cover in this chapter is tracking your progress—and this is where the math creeps back in. When we track our progress on a consistent basis, we're able to see how close we are to achieving the goal we set.

If you want a spreadsheet to follow and complete to make this tracking much easier, please visit www.publishyourpurpose.com/book-extras where you can download the spreadsheet as well as watch an explainer video. I personally use this spreadsheet, and our students in our Getting Started for Authors Program do as well.[26] Having structure around the book-writing process can make or break your success. This is a four-step process, so let's dive in.

STEP 1

Take an inventory of what you have so far. How many words is your current shitty first draft? Write that down.
My shitty first draft is currently 6,300 words.

STEP 2

Recall the number of words you set for your draft goal. Please remember that your word count goal is just an estimate to give you a baseline for your writing plan. It's subject to change by more or fewer words—and that's okay!
My goal is to write a 30,000-word book.

STEP 3

Recall the times you spent writing your draft as it stands now. Now try to remember where you were when you were writing. Were you flying? Sitting at your desk? Hanging out at a local coffee shop? Make whatever notes you can remember. We're going to discuss the power of finding your writing routine in Chapter 9.

This is an important step because when we track our progress and include the details of where we were when we were writing, we can compare

---

26 https://publishyourpurpose.com/writing-support/

> But the reality is that all books start off as shitty first drafts. It's the nature of this process, but sometimes we feel as if we need permission to write something shitty.

that against how many words we wrote that particular session and start to see patterns emerge. This can be a really helpful insight that will make this process feel even more attainable for you.

For example, by tracking my time when I've written my books, I know that when I'm traveling, specifically flying, I'm on fire with writing. I'm able to crank out double, if not triple, the number of words in a short period of time because I'm laser focused.

And now, knowing this about myself, I set the intention that, for every flight I take, I ensure I work on my book in some capacity. While writing the first draft of this book, I know I spent eight flights working on this. I've also tracked the time of day when I write most frequently, which for this book has been at night, whereas previous books have been in the morning.

STEP 4

Now that you have the data on how many words you have so far, how many words you intend to write, and when or where you find yourself in flow most often, you're able to take this spreadsheet and the data in it and further refine your writing plan.

My goal is to write a 30,000-word book.
I have 6,300 words of new content.
I am repurposing 8,900 words of existing content from blog posts and workshops.
I have 14,800 additional words to write.

Bottom Line: You Can Do This!

We began this chapter talking about how there's a formulaic process to getting your book written—and that there are a lot of similarities between your shitty first draft and carving a koi fish ice sculpture. The next step is for you to start taking action toward the plan you set!

In the next chapter, we'll discuss best practices for how to generate new ideas and new content so you can populate the missing holes of your shitty first draft!

GROW FURTHER

Join the Publish Your Purpose 30-Day Book Writing Challenge to create momentum, access accountability, and get one step closer to a rough first draft by having 30 days of writing tips delivered to your inbox daily.

Access the challenge here:
https://publishyourpurpose.com/30-day-book-writing-challenge/.

PROMOTE YOUR PURPOSE

Start Collecting Names

Now is a great time to create a very simple form where you can begin to collect the names of people who've expressed interest in your book. You can use a free email marketing tool like MailChimp, or you can use something as simple as a Google Form. You'll want to collect names and email addresses. You can alert those on this list when you have updates about your book-writing process, whether it's when your manuscript is complete or when you have your book's publication date.

This list will be a pivotal part of your marketing process later. For now, any chance you get to include a link for people to join this list, do it—it will help you grow it faster.

CHAPTER 8
Your First Draft

Yay, you did it! **We're *finally* at the place** in this book where we're going to dive into *actually* writing your first draft! It's taken us a while to get here, but it's my hope that you see the importance of all the prework we did to get to this place.

In the previous chapter, I shared that having an outline is critical to writing your first draft. In general, an outline is imperative for many things, just as it is with a book. But we'll talk about using an outline that's slightly different from what you may be thinking.

Writing Does Not Have to be Linear

From the time we were taught to write, it was ingrained in us that we need to start our story with an introduction, write the body of our text, and then end our story with a conclusion. Whether we were writing a short story in sixth grade or writing a term paper in college, this formula was heavily taught. By default, that's how we're wired to think about writing a book, but the reality is that there's a much more efficient way to do it.

When we read a book we start at the beginning, read the middle, and end at the end. This is a linear process, reading from start to finish. Of course, there are exceptions to this, like when books are intentionally designed to be read in a choose-your-own-adventure style. Because we read linear it's often assumed that we must also write in a linear way—start at Chapter 1 and write through Chapter 18. But that doesn't have to be the case, especially if we have a solid outline to work from.

103

> If we put aside the idea that the writing process must be linear and, instead, write where we're feeling inspired, we can produce more content and in a more efficient way.

If we put aside the idea that the writing process must be linear and, instead, write where we're feeling inspired, we can produce more content and in a more efficient way. An example of this is, as I'm writing this paragraph in my first draft form, this is landing somewhere in Chapter 12, but I do not have Chapters 9–11 written yet. And before writing this, I was working on Chapter 4. My goal has been to write where I'm feeling inspired. And now, as you're reading this final book, this ended up in Chapter 8.

Writing where you're inspired helps you to write where your area of interest is. Of course, this is your book, it's your expertise, and it's the information you know so well, but that does not mean that you're interested in writing it at this exact moment. At this exact moment, for me, I'm not in the mood to write about the publishing process, but I'm interested in writing about how to make this writing process slightly less painful, which is why I'm here with you now.

At some point in this process, you'll have to force yourself to write those last sections that you really don't want to write, because you do need to finish the book eventually; but if you can approach it that way from the start, it can be a lot smoother and less stressful. It's okay to bounce around from idea to idea as long as you're adding more content to the page with each pass and not spinning and spiraling in an unhelpful way. At the time of my writing this chapter, the entire book is written except this chapter and Chapter 10. As you can see, it's very much out of order—but it works!

You may not want to do this, or your personality may not lend itself to this strategy. If this doesn't feel right for you, by all means, keep moving along. I'll continue to say this: this is an individual journey and process, so please take what resonates and leave the rest behind.

PUBLISH YOUR PURPOSE

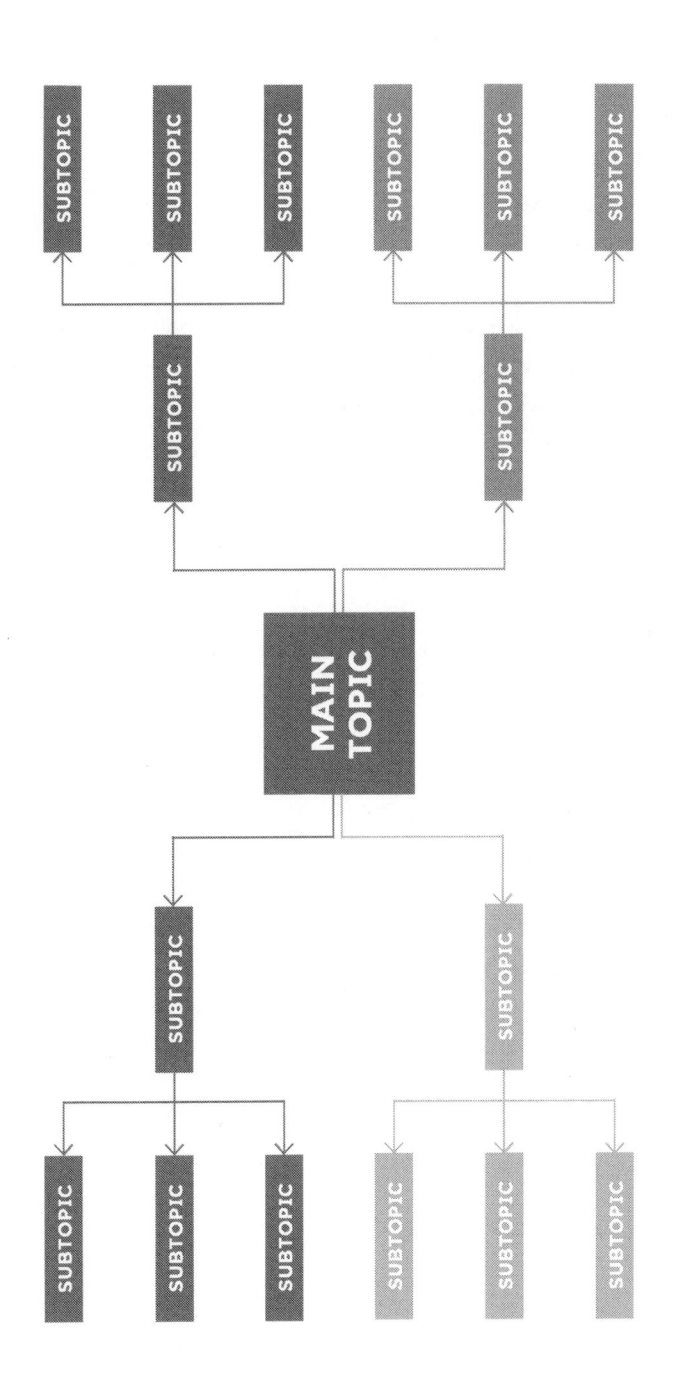

Mind Maps

Before creating an outline, I find mind-mapping to be an incredibly effective and helpful exercise. Many fear the mere thought of coming up with an outline, harkening back to traumatic moments in school of having to write papers. A mind map instead provides room for creativity and flexibility, without the pressure of having anything you write down make sense yet. This is the true definition of the adage, "Throw spaghetti at the wall and see what sticks." While this might not sound like a solid strategy, I assure you it will be—read on.

We must think of this as a two-step process: creating a mind map, then creating an outline. If you're unfamiliar with how a mind map works, it isn't complicated. Let's do one together.

Exercise

Grab something to write on and something to write with. Whatever feels inspiring to you. I like to use a dry-erase board with an assortment of colored markers—you might prefer a napkin and a pen—whatever works! If you're a more visual person and would prefer to watch a video that shows how a mind map is created and/or download a mind map template, you can do so at www.PublishYourPurpose.com/book-extras.

Step 1: Your Central Idea

Your first step is to write down your central idea in the center of what you're writing on—what is your book about? You can write this down in a singular word, a phrase, or a sentence, whatever feels best for you. Circle or box your main idea.

✎ Central idea: a book about how to write and publish a book.

Step 2: Jot Down the Orbiting Ideas

Now, draw lines from your central idea to a new circle or box that's smaller and further from the center of the page. This is going to get messy—and that's okay. It's a natural part of this process. Write down any ideas that come to you related to your book.

- Central idea: a book about how to write and publish a book.
    - Orbiting ideas
        - target readers
        - mindset
        - editing
        - publishing paths

Step 3: Related Ideas

Your mind map should start looking like a spider web with lines and circles extending in all directions from your central idea. Now, make smaller circles and boxes branching off your orbiting ideas from Step 2. At this part in the process, you'll notice your ideas may have started as a single word and will begin to expand into phrases or even sentences.

- Central idea: a book about how to write and publish a book.
    - Orbiting ideas
        - target readers
            - how to narrow down who to write for?
            - how many?
        - mindset
            - imposter syndrome
            - inspiration
            - dealing with author fatigue
        - editing
            - phases of the editing process
            - when to engage an editor
            - editing best practices
        - publishing paths
            - types of publishers
            - time vs. money
            - who's in control?

You can see this in both the mind map view (before we started Step 1) and now in a more linear view as I've bullet-pointed it out due to the nature of this book. You may gravitate to writing things in list form versus a creative mind map, and that's totally fine. The purpose here is to do something that works for you, something that allows you to throw ideas on paper in a stream-of-conscious way without thinking about the interconnectivity of it all yet. None of this has to make any sense right now, and I can assure you that if you show someone else what you've just done, it will make zero sense—and that's perfect!

Step 4: Just Keep Adding

The benefit of a mind map is that you can keep doing this over and over, circle by circle, until you're feeling complete and like you've exhausted the ideas that are in your head. I encourage you to put it away for 24 hours and come back to it this time tomorrow, with a fresh set of eyes.

Step 5: Fresh Eyes

Now that you've had some time and space from your mind map, you might be looking at it and wondering, *What the heck was I thinking?!* This is also a good sign. It means you've purged what's in your head, which is allowing for new ideas to flow in. If you're enjoying the mind-mapping exercise, you're welcome to do this for a few rounds until you feel complete. Then, we'll move on to putting this into an outline.

Creating an Outline

The next phase of this process is turning your mind map into an outline that you can begin writing against. We're going to follow another multi-step process to get our outline created.

Step 1: Group Your Thoughts Together

The first step is to group like-minded thoughts. As you scan the many ideas circled on your mind map, see if there are easy ways to group your ideas together. How you group them is up to you, but think about how you would teach this information, which will give you an indication of how you might want to group them. At the end of the day, your book is a teaching tool intended for people to learn from, so putting your thoughts into groups is the best first step. You may find that a lot of your ideas actually belong in multiple different groups. Great! Put your ideas in as many groups as they feel like they fit. If your mind map has 50 items on the page, see if you can pair it down to 10 groups that have a theme to them. Don't worry about balance. You may have one group that has 21 items in it and another group with three. There's no right or wrong—and all of this will be further refined later.

Step 2: Put Meat on the Bones

Now that you have these lists of groups that are thematically driven, what you have are the bones of your chapters. At this point, this should be in some kind of list form. Your next task is to write down as many new ideas that weren't previously captured in this list. Really brainstorm and just data dump without thinking about the how just yet. Don't get in your head about how you're going to write this, or how you're going to connect the dots between all of these thoughts—that's a future you situation.

Step 3: Convert to Chapters

This is where it could feel scary, but try to let that emotion move through you. At this step, you'll want to assign your groupings of bullet points a chapter title. This is intended for inspirational purposes. If it feels like too much pressure for you, then keep it in a loose, bullet-point list. But what's beautiful is you should start to see your chapter-by-chapter outline emerging from a very chaotic mind map exercise.

Next to your main heading for your groupings, write in a sentence or two what this section would be about. Put a chapter number next to it, but know that this will change 90 times before you get to your first draft, and that is 100 percent part of this process. The outline for this book has changed more times than I can count and, even as I write this, my Chapters 9 and 10 are somewhat of a hot mess of ideas. It's the nature of the beast.

Step 4: Come Back Later

The best thing you can do is sleep on this. Before you start writing, put away your outline for 24 hours and come back to it with a fresh mind. Repeat all of the steps from this chapter as many times as you need to, to feel like you've exhausted your ideas and that you've captured as much as you can in this outline. This isn't intended to be complicated, so try to approach this with a mindset of simplicity. This document is for your eyes only. No one is seeing it. No one is judging you for it. Trust me, if you saw my early drafts and outlines you would certainly have opinions about me and my abilities to teach you this process. No one is immune to this process; we all have to go through it.

Your Shitty First Draft

In the previous chapter I granted you permission to write a shitty first draft. Know that your outline and your first draft are both going to be shitty, and they are going to morph and change over time. The key is being okay with this not being your best work.

Remember the person carving the ice sculpture. If they graded themselves on how their sculpture looked when they first started the process, they wouldn't feel like an artist and would feel defeated. Don't do that to yourself. As hard as it may be, especially for the Type A folks out there, try to just be okay with how things are. It's going to be shitty—and that's okay.

You now have a first draft outline, albeit potentially a shitty one, but you have an outline. This means you can start populating your outline to create that shitty first draft. At this point in the book, you know what your word count goal is and you have a writing schedule in place. The next step is to start putting words on paper!

A Sample Outline

Right now your outline might feel like a word jumble in which there's a lot happening but none of it is making sense. You have the freedom and autonomy to do whatever you want to do to get this draft written. But you might be thinking practically and wondering what a book outline could look like. There are *many* ways you can construct a non-fiction book. On the following pages you'll find a sample outline that you could add to your previous bullet points.

Introduction: The Problem

- Opening story to introduce the concept of this book
- Inspiring vision of what's possible with the book
- Background story—why should the reader trust that you know what you're talking about?
- What the reader can expect if they use/apply the info in this book
- How the book is organized (brief chapter-by-chapter overview)
- How to use this book/exercises
- What you hope for the reader as they dive into the book

Chapter 1: Introduce the Solution

- Opening story—what your/a client's life was like before they did what you're suggesting.
- Topic #1: why should they do what you suggest?
- Topic #2: overview of how to do it, the details of which will be explained in the chapters that follow.
- Topic #3: what they need to know to get started.
- Exercises/Practices
- Conclusion/Transition to next chapter

Chapter 2: Step One Toward the Solution

- Opening story—choose one that represents what it looks like when your reader does what you're suggesting.
- Overview of chapter theme
- Topic #1:
- Topic #2:
- Topic #3:
- Exercises/Practices
- Conclusion/Transition to next chapter

Chapter 3: Step Two Toward the Solution

- Opening story
- Overview of chapter theme
- Topic #1:
- Topic #2:
- Topic #3:
- Exercises/Practices
- Conclusion/Transition to next chapter

Chapter 4: Step Three Toward the Solution

- Opening story
- Overview of chapter theme
- Topic #1:
- Topic #2:
- Topic #3:
- Exercises/Practices
- Conclusion/Transition to next chapter

Chapter 5: Step Four Toward the Solution

- Opening story
- Overview of chapter theme
- Topic #1:
- Topic #2:
- Topic #3:
- Exercises/Practices
- Conclusion/Transition to next chapter

Chapter 6: Next Step or Subtopic

- Opening story
- Overview of chapter theme
- Topic #1:
- Topic #2:
- Topic #3:
- Exercises/Practices
- Conclusion/Transition to next chapter

Chapter 7: Next Step or Subtopic

- Opening Story
- Overview of chapter theme
- Topic #1:
- Topic #2:
- Topic #3:
- Exercises/Practices
- Conclusion/Transition to next chapter

Chapter 8: Next Step or Subtopic

- Opening Story
- Overview of chapter theme
- Topic #1:
- Topic #2:
- Topic #3
- Exercises/Practices
- Conclusion/Transition to next chapter

Conclusion/Chapter 9: How Readers Use This Information Moving Forward in Their Lives

- Overview of chapter theme—you can go big-picture, high-level in this last chapter to set up the "what's next" for the reader.
- Topic #1:
- Topic #2:
- Topic #3:
- Vision for the reader

You can see that there's nothing complex about this sample. It's a very simple formula of introducing the problem, discussing the solution, then chipping away at it in a series of steps.

If this outline looks helpful to you, I encourage you to use it. If it doesn't resonate, leave it behind. If you're feeling that having a sample like this will help you, then head over to Google and type in "non-fiction book outline" and you'll get a lot of results to choose from. Pick something that feels good to you. If you're fine with your previous bullet-point list, stick with that—don't overcomplicate it. If you'd like to download this outline, you can do so at www.PublishYourPurpose.com/book-extras.

Scrivener [Not a paid endorsement]

There's a writing program called Scrivener that I've been a huge proponent of for the last decade. I started using it when I was writing my second book back in 2013. I personally love this program so much that we include a license for our students in our Getting Started for Authors writing program. There are numerous benefits to this program, but I'm going to highlight a few as they relate to the rest of our discussion in this chapter.

As we just covered, writing doesn't have to be linear. The challenge, though, is that all default programs on our computers or phones are designed in a linear fashion. What happens when you open up a Word document? It opens to Page 1. What happens when we open a Google Doc or Pages? They open to Page 1. So even if you set the intention to write where you're inspired and in a nonlinear way, the programs available to us are not designed that way.

Scrivener appears to have been originally designed for fiction and is used widely by fiction writers. With fiction, there are things like storylines, plot points, and character details to worry about, which we don't have to deal with in non-fiction. As a result of this added functionality, I use maybe 5 percent of what this program offers, and it has 100 percent changed my life as it relates to writing. And not just books, either. Here are the top three Scrivener benefits.

Benefit 1

The primary benefit of Scrivener is that it prevents us from going down the rabbit hole of linear thinking. You can open your file and jump to any area you please with no impact on the existing content you've written.

It also provides a place to put *all* of your content—the content we discussed repurposing in Chapter 7. If you have blog posts, articles, newsletters, emails, proposals—truly anything—it gives you the space to drop the information in and see it from a 30,000-foot view. When you can see it from a high level, you have a better sense of what's already there versus what may be missing. It's much harder scrolling through a 200-page Word document to determine whether you already wrote what you're about to write.

The benefit here is that you can drag all of that content into this program and have it all at your fingertips, which is a very different experience from trying to do this in a Word, Google, or Pages document. Often we're pulling in content but don't actually know where it fits yet. In a Word document, you drop it wherever you think it might belong at that moment, but the reality is that you might change your mind six times before it lands in its final destination. With Scrivener you can put the content in two places, or even three. You can scatter it to where you think it may make sense and then easily remove it later without worrying about accidental duplication in your long document.

I've personally saved so much time simply by *not* accidentally pasting a paragraph in the wrong location of my Google Doc. Have you done that before? You're on Page 85 and see a paragraph that belongs on Page 22, so you highlight and cut that paragraph and scroll for three minutes to Page 22, only to realize you accidentally pasted part of it onto Page 63. You didn't realize it, so now you have to hit undo, undo, undo, but you've accidentally undone a great paragraph in a different area that you had just written. And before you know it, 30 minutes have gone down the drain and you have nothing to show for it.

If this hasn't happened to you, I applaud you. Because for me, this has happened more times than I care to admit. Though we accept manuscripts in various formats, PYP internally works exclusively within Google Docs, so this happens frequently enough in small 10–15-page documents. But it's even more frustrating when it's an 80+ page manuscript. Scrivener avoids *all* of this for you.

Benefit 2

The second biggest benefit I see with Scrivener is from a self-editing standpoint. Because we read in a linear fashion, we have a tendency to also write linearly, which means we also have a tendency to edit in a linear fashion by starting at Page 1 and working our way through Page 90. The challenge with this is that every time you open up that

Word document, you're back on Page 1 and somehow find something to change, tweak, or edit, rather than getting back to Page 76 where you left off the day before. This creates imbalanced manuscripts in which the first few chapters, or even the first half of the book, are in significantly better shape because they've been self-edited way more times than the content in the middle or the end of the document.

Even if we have every intention of focusing and opening that Pages document on Chapter 4 and editing from where we left off, it almost becomes a compulsion where we *have* to stop along the way because we see red or green squiggly lines beneath our words. They yell at us that we've spelled something wrong or that we don't know how to construct a proper sentence. This is a distraction to the task at hand, which is to get to Chapter 4 and edit or start writing for Chapter 5. Why not bypass all of that unnecessary chaos?

Benefit 3

The best part about this program is that it has continued to remain affordable for most people. At the time of writing this book, the price point is under $50 for a license.

Tutorial

Rather than fangirling over this program and taking up extra space, I invite you to check out a video walkthrough that we use with our writing students. It gives you a high-level sense of how the program works, and you'll be able to see with your own eyes how transformational the writing process can be with a program like this. And the example I use in that video tutorial is from this book, so it'll be another opportunity to see what a shit show disaster my draft was before it became the finished book you're reading right now. You can access the video walkthrough here: www.PublishYourPurpose.com/book-extras.

Don't Censor Yourself

The last thing to think about in relation to your first draft is censorship. We'll cover censorship by others in Chapter 13, but here I'm talking about you standing in your own way.

When we're thinking about the first draft of our manuscript, we're often so focused on who's going to be reading it and who's going to be editing it that we hold back from saying the things that we want or need to say. We censor ourselves. We think so far forward about who may judge us from what we've written that we're constantly battling that inner critic and censoring every word or every sentence on the page. This is like walking into quicksand. We think things like,

- *I can't possibly share that story, it's too personal;*
- *If I share that story, my clients will see me in a different light;* and
- *If I claim to be an expert on this topic and then admit to not knowing what I'm doing, I will lose clients or won't gain new ones.*

Fun fact on that last one—if this were the reason they weren't going to work with you, chances are they wouldn't have worked with you to begin with. When I published my memoir, *House on Fire* in September 2020, I had all of these thoughts and then some. I was genuinely concerned that those I work with wouldn't look at me the same way. It took me a solid year to work through the anxiety that was coming up for me. I've had nothing but positive feedback, despite my memoir sharing some of my darkest times that feel incredibly vulnerable and exposing.

This can be incredibly difficult to work through, but your goal should be to write as if no one is watching. We all love the motto, "Dance like no one is watching." This is the same—just write your heart out. Don't think about who may read it later and what they may think of you. You'll have a lot of time between now and when the book is published to work through all of those emotions and potentially edit your writing as a result.

Depending on what you're writing, you could approach this the same way you would write a journal. When writing a journal you don't censor yourself, you just write it down, knowing (or having some level of confidence) that no one else will be reading this work. Just get it out there.

We don't want to be living in a scarcity mindset when it comes to getting words on the page; we want to be living in full abundance. We'll dive into the editing process in more detail in Chapter 10, where you'll see how your book draft will not be published without many eyes on it to ensure all of these worries and concerns are appropriately handled.

Bottom Line: You Can Do This!

Having an outline for your book is a critical part of this journey. You now have the skills you need to create an outline and begin populating content. You also have peace of mind knowing that, when you sit down to write, you can jump into any area of your outline without worrying, *Where do I begin today?* In the next chapter, we're going to talk about the power of finding your writing routine and the benefits that brings.

> We think so far forward about who may judge us from what we've written that we're constantly battling that inner critic and censoring every word or every sentence on the page.

PROMOTE YOUR PURPOSE

Make a List of Related Podcasts

Podcasts are an incredible means of promoting a new book. If you're a podcast listener, you'll no doubt have heard someone promoting their book on a show you listen to. If you aren't a podcast listener, you don't need to become one, but you'll want to leverage them as much as you can.

Take time to explore podcasts related to your topic and begin to compile them into a list. You'll reach out to the podcasts on this list once you have a publication date for your book, to request to be a guest on their show.

GROW
FURTHER

Join the Publish Your Purpose 30-Day Book Writing Challenge to create momentum, access accountability, and get one step closer to a rough first draft by having 30 days of writing tips delivered to your inbox daily.

Access the challenge here:
https://publishyourpurpose.com/30-day-book-writing-challenge/.

CHAPTER 9
Adding Ease to Your Writing Process

In this chapter we'll cover how to create a writing routine that works for you, how to overcome the doubt around your shitty first draft, and what some top writing strategies are that will help you in completing your first draft.

In the previous few chapters, we discussed shitty first drafts and the power that can come from giving yourself permission to be okay with it not being the best right out of the gate. This topic is repeated here because it's just that important, from both the emotional and mental health sides of this process. So before we talk about creating a concrete writing routine, let's further dive into imposter syndrome when it comes to writing a shitty first draft.

If you're a thought leader in any way, whether you have a platform of five or 50,000, you've likely experienced the stress of feeling like your work isn't good enough. Whether you felt like the speech you gave just didn't hit the right note or that your recent blog post wasn't strong enough, these are the results of a constant striving for perfection that simply isn't attainable.

Your imposter syndrome might go deeper, as it does for many of us, where there are a series of questions playing on repeat in your head:

- *Who am I to write this book?*
- *Why would anyone want to listen to me?*
- *Who cares about my past experiences?*
- *Who cares about my story?*

- *Why does anyone want to hear what I have to say about my profession, career, or business?*
- *Who says I'm the expert?*

These questions can be endless, and they serve no purpose—other than making us feel inadequate, which can derail the entire book project. But we can move past our feelings of being an imposter. We can really elevate both our moods and our production, and we can become more efficient and more effective so that we really can crank out a lot of words and get that first draft written.

If you can acknowledge the imposter in the room, set them aside, and move on to better things, you'll be able to complete your shitty first draft and feel triumphant in doing so. Focus on what you can uniquely do, and let your imposter go take a nap somewhere while you continue to write.

I've always had a Type A tendency in my life, especially in business. When I do something, I go *all* in. I'm not sure how to function with just half of my ass involved in something. But one area I've gotten pretty good at letting go is in writing, because I've seen how stressful it can be to be striving for something that's unattainable unless you give up something in the process.

Your first draft isn't a singular first draft. It's a combination of *many* drafts and is what you hand over to an editor or a publisher. But leading up to that first draft you'll have many others. For example, I have 41 drafts at the time of this writing—and I'm not even ready to submit my "first draft" to an editor yet. That's 41 passes at carving away at the ice sculpture we talked about in Chapter 7.

Continuing to be Type A, as much as I've been working on moving away from that, I cringe at the thought of even handing over the draft I'm currently writing. Why? Because it's not perfect. It's not up to my standards. As a multi-book author, I feel it should be better. As a publisher, I feel it should be perfect. The editors who will work on this book work on other authors' books that my company publishes, so the thought of them seeing my raw work feels cringeworthy.

> Your first draft isn't a singular first draft. It's a combination of *many* drafts and is what you hand over to an editor or a publisher.

But guess what? The writing and editing processes are both inherently messy. Editors and publishing professionals are accustomed to receiving work that isn't in the best shape from the onset, but it's their job to elevate it, to make it better. So rather than spend endless hours stressing about whether what you're writing is perfect, first focus on getting that shitty first draft complete.

That shitty first draft will be the ice sculpture that resembles a koi fish, but it will be missing a lot of detail. In the next chapter, we'll talk more about the editing process and what to do to prepare your manuscript for an editor, but for now I want you to let the reins go. I want you to relax and settle into the fact that you're not perfect and neither is your writing—and that's exactly how this process should be.

We've all heard the adage or seen a meme that speaks to the fact that we would never talk to a friend the way we talk to ourselves, and there's a lot of truth to that. Now let's drop the pretenses and embrace our shitty first draft by creating a writing routine that inspires you to get this draft completed!

Writing Routines

In Chapter 6 we discussed a writing schedule as part of the foundation of your writing plan. Reference your workbook to remind yourself of what you decided your writing schedule would be. (If you haven't downloaded it by now, what are you waiting for? Get it at www.PublishYourPurpose.com/book-extras.) Did you commit to writing one hour per day, four days a week? Or did you commit to writing once a week for one hour? Whatever you decided, now is a good time to evaluate that goal. Does what you decided three chapters ago still feel good for you now? If so, great! If not, time to modify.

A writing schedule is exactly what it sounds like, it's a schedule. A writing routine, while it sounds like a schedule, it's an enhancement to the process. It's imperative to create a routine and ritual that will help you get into a rhythm where you feel inspired and productive. Here are some questions to ponder:

ADDING EASE TO YOUR WRITING PROCESS

- What time of day do you like writing?
- What type of environment do you like to be in?
- Do you prefer to be at a bustling coffee shop with ambient noise?
- Do you prefer to have noise-canceling headphones while working in a library?
- Are you listening to music?
- What type of lighting do you like?
- What type of drink do you want nearby?
- Is there some specific type of clothing you want to be wearing?
- Are there certain smells surrounding you?

Finding a routine and ritual can have many benefits. The first is that you've created an environment where you're comfortable, where you feel good, and where you feel inspired. This is a much better scenario than approaching this writing process as a chore and being miserable and uncomfortable from start to finish. This can and should be a joyous process at times, but we need to be intentional about that if we want to make that happen.

What works for one person won't work for another, so while it's good to talk to others who are also writing books, sticking with something that you know will work for you will be for the best. Personally, I can't write and be creative if I'm sitting at my desk. I need to be on my laptop and mobile. For me, traveling is where I'm in my zone of genius and can crank out thousands of words effortlessly. But the drawback is that if I'm not flying often (ahem, COVID-19) my productivity can slow down. I began writing this book in the summer of 2020, when flying was not an option. And if I look at my progress tracker spreadsheet, I can see that I started writing in July and put it down a couple of months later in September. A similar thing happened in 2021. I wrote from May to July and then stopped. I still wasn't traveling then. Then my first flight in years happened on August 1, 2022, and I was reignited.

This book was truly written between August 2022 and February 2023 because I got my mojo back. I didn't try to force it; I was patient and waited for the inspiration to strike. This may not be an option for you. You may have a pressing need to get your book done immediately and don't have time to wait for inspiration. What we can do in lieu of that is come up with a writing routine and ritual that creates inspiration.

Even if it doesn't feel inspiring at first, even if you still feel like it's a bit of a slog at first, even if you feel like you're forcing yourself to be inspired at first—it's all okay! The beautiful thing that begins to happen is that you get into a routine. A routine that when you hear a certain song, your mind knows it's time to start writing (for me, Leonard Cohen's albums *Old Ideas* and *You Want It Darker* were both instrumental—no pun intended—in keeping me focused while writing in busy environments). A routine that when you smell a certain candle, your mind knows it's time to start writing. A routine that when you're wearing a certain oversized sweatshirt, your mind knows it's time to start writing.

It's magical when this happens—and it works. Of the previous six books I wrote, the majority of those were written at a coffee shop down the street from me. I would go in, grab a decaf, turn my Wi-Fi off, and listen to the modern jazz music playing in the background. Because I had trained my brain to get into a creative mode when I walked through those doors, when I sat down I was primed and ready to put words on the page. It's a habit we're continually developing that can make a big impact on our productivity.

We've all heard of writer's block and we've probably all experienced it too. But when you have a routine and ritual and solidify that into the form of a habit, the sky's the limit. The writer's block that may have once prevented you from getting a single word on the page will suddenly dissipate within 5–10 minutes of getting into your routine.

The Pomodoro Technique

Years ago, I learned about the Pomodoro technique from a business coach. This is a very simple concept, and you can modify it to whatever degree feels good for you. Essentially, a Pomodoro is to be viewed as a writing sprint. Block out one hour of time, and set a timer for 55 minutes. Turn off all distractions. Close everything down on your computer that isn't necessary, turn off Wi-Fi—literally everything—and make this time as distraction-free as possible. When those 55 minutes are up, take a break for 5 minutes to check your emails, check social media, go to the bathroom, stretch your legs, grab some water—anything to move your body for just a few minutes.

You can do this as 25 minutes of writing with a 5-minute break, or you can do 40 minutes of writing with a 20-minute break. Whatever works for you. But the goal is to intentionally plan breaks so you can be laser focused while you're actually writing. When you have specific break times built in, it will help you become increasingly more efficient in your process because you'll be less distracted.

Motivation and Rewards

Treating yourself can be a good motivator. We use rewards as a way to get our children, coworkers, or employees to do something that needs to get done, so why not incentivize yourself? The first step is to reference your original writing schedule and validate whether it's reasonable. If you said you were going to write seven days a week, is that reasonable? If you said four days a week, is that reasonable? Just ensure that what you've set for yourself is attainable before proceeding.

Now that you've reconfirmed your writing schedule, brainstorm how you might incentivize yourself to stay motivated and on track. What motivates you in general? How are you celebrating the little wins that are compounding over the process of writing your book?

- Do you enjoy physical gifts?
- Do you enjoy experiences?
- Do you enjoy spending time with others?

Whatever it may be for you, find a way to reward yourself no matter how silly it might feel. We worked with an author once who bought a sheet of gold stars and would give herself a gold star after every writing session. When she hit a certain amount, she would treat herself with a manicure. For her, that was a motivator.

> We've all heard of writer's block and we've probably all experienced it too. But when you have a routine and ritual and solidify that into the form of a habit, the sky's the limit.

I'm more of an experience type of person, so my motivation is knowing that once I hit the goal I set for myself for that particular time frame, I will do something physically active. In the case of writing Chapters 8, 9, and 10 of this book, I committed to writing one chapter per night for three nights in a row, before leaving for a ski trip in Vail. My motivation to get these chapters done allowed me to have the time and space to not stress about what I didn't do before I left for vacation.

Yours could be that every time you write a chapter you add $5 to a jar to save up for something that you've deemed is totally frivolous but want it anyway, and this is the way to keep you motivated. Be creative here and do what feels good. Then ask yourself how this makes you feel. If it's working, keep doing it; if it isn't, reevaluate and see what you might be able to do differently.

Top Writing Strategies

The word *strategy* often implies that something is complicated or sophisticated, and many strategies are. But sometimes some of the simplest strategies can have the biggest impact on writing.

Turn Off Spell Check

One of the best strategies I began employing years ago was turning off grammar and spell check. If you use Scrivener, this is even easier.

We've all been taught to rely on and/or leverage tools such as spell check and grammar check from whichever word processing program we're writing within. Most of the time, this is a great idea. It helps us write more powerful and coherent content.

But when it comes to writing your manuscript, turning off those exact tools designed to help you can be one of the best things you can do to stay in the flow. Finding your flow in writing can mean the difference between writing 200 words and 2,000 words in a single writing session. Being in flow is incredible if you can find a way to harness it.

Here's what happens to me whether I'm writing an email or this book: I write a sentence, and halfway through I see the red squiggly line showing me I've spelled something wrong. So then I stop, go back to fix the misspelled word, and knock myself out of flow because I'm no longer typing but rather mousing back and forth to adjust that one word.

It takes practice to just roll with it and stay in the flow, but it can be a huge timesaver in the long run. I like to write a couple of paragraphs and then go back and fix my mistakes, whether they are spelling or grammar. You can also write an entire chapter, an entire section, or just one paragraph at a time. The point is to not stop and fix each and every sentence. This will help you stay in flow longer and produce more content more quickly.

You'll definitely have an alarmed moment when you look back up at your screen and realize it's in a sea of green and red from the mistakes that you've made, but you can quickly address everything at once versus stopping and starting at every sentence. Definitely make sure you're looking up at your screen frequently just to make sure that your hands are on the right keys on the keyboard. I've made that mistake a few times myself; somehow I had shifted my hands a hair to the left and typed a bunch of nonsense.

This will feel uncomfortable at first—but that's okay. The entire process of writing a book can be incredibly uncomfortable, so this is just par for the course.

Use Interviews

Interviews can be a powerful tool for generating new content for your book. This can be especially true as you're trying to determine how to best tell your story as it relates to the content that you're teaching and/or explaining to your reader. It can be tricky to know what part of your story to include versus what not to include. It can also be hard to know how to tell your story in general so that it makes sense for your reader.

Using interviews can be an efficient tool in this process. The steps you'll want to take are 1) prepare the questions, 2) have someone who knows you really well interview you, and 3) have someone who you've recently just met interview you. The balance of having two perspectives can help you get to the heart of what to include.

Let's define an interview for a moment—what I mean here is having someone ask you a series of questions that you're recording using some sort of voice memo app on your phone or a program such as Zoom. You don't have to record the conversation if you're really good at remembering. But why not record it to have it, since recording is so readily accessible to everyone? I remember back in the day (the late '90s/early '00s) when you had to intentionally purchase a device that would allow you to record a conversation. Now it's always available to us.

Your first step is to prepare a list of questions that you'll want to have the person ask you. This might seem silly to have someone ask you questions that you could just write the answers to yourself, but the reality is that how you answer those questions when you're sitting at your screen and writing are likely going to be different from how you would answer them in a conversation. Most of us, when being asked a question, will provide more descriptive detail and remember more than if we're typing alone.

The second step is starting with the person who knows you well. Find someone who knows your story. If you're trying to include a lot of personal stories, ask someone to do this with you who knows you in that way. If you're trying to include a lot of your professional story, find someone who knows you in that way.

The huge benefit of having someone who knows you well ask you questions is that they'll know when you aren't going deep enough. You'll hear them say things like, "Well, what about the time you did...?" or "Weren't you part of that project that would tie into what you're writing about?" They'll know your story in a way that they'll be able to poke holes in what you're saying and/or force you to elaborate on details that you may have forgotten about. This helps build out a more comprehensive and robust story to include in your book.

When taking the third step, which is working with someone who doesn't know you super well, you'll get a totally different benefit. Because this person doesn't know you well, they don't know the intimate details of your story or what you're writing about. The value here is that they'll ask questions and be looking for information that you may have glossed over because you believed it wasn't relevant. But the new person, the new ear, will see holes that you can fill, essentially being reflective of your reader. Often we just dive right into the heart of a story without properly teeing up and/or introducing it. A new person interviewing you will help you not miss those critical pieces of the story.

If you schedule 30 or 60 minutes to do this, you'll find that you have a lot of content to work with. For me and the pace at which I speak, I know that a 60-minute audio recording equals about 9,000 words of content. That's not to say that this will all be usable, because it won't be. You'll need to smooth it out, pull the pieces from each interview, and find a way to round out what you're saying. But it'll be a heck of a lot easier working from a transcribed conversation than working in a vacuum completely independent.

Add Your Story Later

Building upon what we just discussed regarding having people interview you to help you tell your story, a strong way to approach this process is to add your story later. If you're struggling with telling your story in relation to your chapters, you can focus on the teaching aspect of what you're doing first, then overlay your story.

If we go back to thinking about the koi fish ice sculpture, this would be another pass in the first draft creation process. You'll essentially have your book written in a way that's doing all of the teaching. Then you can review it in detail and see where you can add your story after the fact. This doesn't have to be complicated and can work very well. You can also tackle this in the self-editing part of the process, which we'll talk about in the next chapter.

Write Stand-Alone Chapters

Out of the strategies provided, this is the most complex. This strategy spans the writing process but can also have a big impact on marketing your book later.

Years ago I was listening to a podcast with Tim Ferris, author of *The 4-Hour Work Week*, *The 4-Hour Body*, and *The 4-Hour Chef*. He was explaining his process, which was to write every chapter as if it could independently stand on its own. This is good for both the writing and the marketing of your book. Let's go through the primary benefits of doing this.

1. When you're approaching each chapter as an individual piece of content that can stand on its own, it makes the entire process more simplified. Rather than determining how you're going to write 30,000 words, your focus needs to be, *How can I write this one chapter that's 1,000 or 3,000 words?* Writing 1,000–3,000 words is a lot less overwhelming than writing 30,000.

2. If you're using existing content from your business or profession, this can help define explicitly where you'll use your existing content. You can assess high-level and decide what the chapter is going to be about, gather the existing content you've already created, and then poke holes to see where content is missing. You'll be able to brainstorm, mind map, create an outline around what you're missing, and construct the rest of your chapter.

3. When thinking of how you'll market your book down the road, having your chapters act as stand-alone pieces can make your marketing process so much easier. There's a general rule of thumb with book marketing that you can give away 40 percent of your content without it impacting the reader's desire to purchase your book. Not consecutively, however. For example, you may want to provide Chapter 2 to one publication as an exclusive excerpt from your book and Chapter 5 to a different media outlet. When you write your chapters in a stand-alone type of way, these opportunities become much simpler to execute.

You would never want to provide Chapters 1 through 4 to one publication because that could impact your sales, but you could give away four separate chapters to four separate places. When I was launching one of my past non-fiction books, *But You Don't Look Gay*, I gave Chapter 2 to Lesbian.com as an exclusive piece that they then shared and promoted to their readers. That then helped me get new listeners to my podcast, subscribers to my blog, and sales to my book. They also promoted this on the home page of their website. Because that chapter had been written as a stand-alone piece, it was really easy to arrange this promotion with them.

This strategy can have a full-circle impact. Obviously, there will be editing work that needs to be done that will help you identify how to bridge your chapters together and create cohesion across your book. But that's the next phase of this process, not right now while you're in the content-generating phase of getting the first draft of your manuscript written.

Not all books are written like this, but I do find it easier to market them when it's done this way. Writing a book is a solo journey and there are a lot of ways that this can be done. Some books are written in such an intertwined way that even pulling a few paragraphs for marketing purposes can be tricky because there isn't enough context to the content being pulled. Others allow for this flawlessly. Regardless of whether you use this strategy to get your book written, it's worth thinking about areas of your book you can pull from for future marketing. This can be done very simply by adding comments and/or highlights in your manuscript as you continue through the writing process.

Do Market Research

As authors, we often don't do enough market or competitive research. You may know off the top of your head what books exist that are similar to yours, but you may not know them intimately—at least to a degree that can help serve you and your readers better.

Dedicate some time to researching Amazon. Yes, Amazon, simply because that's where you'll find the most reviews of any online book retailer. Find a couple of books that are similar to yours and go to the reviews section. See what readers are saying about that book. Read both the 5-star reviews and the 1-star reviews. If you're seeing that readers are outraged because of the way an author phrased a problem or solution, make note of it. If you see that readers are in love with a solution to a problem, make note of it. Maybe you'll see that readers love the author because of their authentic voice and life experiences; make note of it.

What you want to consider is how you can modify the direction of your book as a result of both the positive and the negative feedback you've found on books similar to yours. This will heighten your awareness of the market of readers, and it'll help you align your message, your content, and your writing.

What you may also get more insights on is how your book description may end up. What is your book about? What are their books about? Where is there overlap and where is there difference? Do these reviews give you insights on how to further differentiate yours in a way that will help capture an audience of readers who haven't been satisfied with books of similar nature?

Consistency of Voice

Sticking with your natural writing style can make all the difference in the world for getting your draft onto paper in a more streamlined way. In addition to writing in a linear way being beaten into us from an early age, writing in a certain style or tone has been as well. The path of least resistance is to write in your natural writing style. If you naturally write in a conversational way, write in a conversational way. If you naturally write in a more academic way, write in a more academic way.

You'll want to go back and reference who you're writing for to ensure that your writing style will align with their expectations. Given that it does, writing in a way that comes naturally to you'll be more effective across the board. As you've experienced throughout this book, I write in a conversational way. Had I been forced, or forced myself, into writing this book in a more academic way, it never would have been written.

Then, whichever style you have chosen—be consistent in that style. Don't shake things up midway through because you're feeling bored with your own writing. Readers value consistency. The value of consistency with regards to the structure and flow of a chapter, to the tone in which you write it, even to the length of your chapters—it's an underrated area of the writing process. Be consistent.

Have a Parking Lot

The final tip that can add ease to your writing process is having a "parking lot" where you can put down the ideas that come to you while you're writing. If you've ever been in a planning meeting within the organization that you may own or work for, it's very common to have the easel and flip chart in the corner of the room to jot down notes that aren't relevant to the conversation at hand but are important enough not to be forgotten.

This can also tremendously help with your book because you might be writing about one area and, instead of knocking yourself out of the flow to focus on another area, you can drop it in your parking lot document and move on. Then you can dedicate time during the process to come back and review your parking lot list and decide where the information should go, if anywhere. This concept prevents you from waking up in the middle of the night with an idea that you thought of earlier in the day but did nothing with.

If you're using a program like Scrivener, you can create a file and call it "notes" or "ideas," or simply call it the "parking lot." If you're writing in a Word document, I encourage you to have this be a separate file from your manuscript itself. That way it's a short document where you can easily find what your ideas were, without the need for a lot of scrolling.

File > Save As

Before we celebrate that you have a shitty first draft, have you saved your draft recently? Have you done a File > Save As recently? There's nothing like losing your work when you're close to the finish line. At my first office job in 2004, I had been working on a file for over two weeks when the program I was using (remember Quark?) crashed. Even though I had been hitting Save on the file multiple times a day for 15 days straight, it didn't matter, because that one file was corrupted. Because of that one incident, for the last two decades I have made it a habit to do a File > Save As at the end of every writing session—sometimes twice in one session—simply because I don't want to take the chance of having a corrupted file. Is this extreme? Yes. But does it bring me peace of mind? Also yes.

At this moment of writing, I have 52 saved files for this manuscript—and I haven't even exported this into Google Docs yet to begin the self-editing process. It's better to be safe than sorry, even if it borders on neurosis.

Bottom Line: You Can Do This!

There are many ways to add ease to your writing process. This chapter scratched just the surface. I encourage you to explore other writing hacks that work for you and your process. We often don't know what works for us until we try! Here's your opportunity to be creative and explore.

GROW FURTHER

Join the Publish Your Purpose 30-Day Book Writing Challenge to create momentum, access accountability, and get one step closer to a rough first draft by having 30 days of writing tips delivered to your inbox daily.

Access the challenge here:
www.publishyourpurpose.com/30-day-book-writing-challenge.

PROMOTE YOUR PURPOSE

Make a List of Blogs

Blogs, similar to podcasts, can be a great way to promote an upcoming book. Look for guest blogging opportunities in your space. Take time to research high-quality blogs that are already written for the audience your book is intended for. This is a chance to leverage an audience that someone else has already built.

You'll want to be mindful of what value you can bring to this blogger's audience (same for podcasters), so their chances of saying yes to you being a guest blogger (or guest on a podcast) are much higher. We must always think about the intended recipient of our message and ensure that our message is aligned with their values, so we can feel confident knowing there is mutual benefit to both us and the audience we are interacting with.

CHAPTER 10
What to Know About Editing

In Chapter 8, we talked about your first draft and how it most likely will be shitty, because that's just how this process works. I hope by now you've gotten comfortable with that concept. But the good news is it won't remain that way! What a relief, right? In this chapter, we're going to talk about what you can do to self-edit your manuscript before handing it off to a professional editor. Then we'll talk about the types of editors, their roles, and how to prepare for the next steps in the publishing process.

Importance of Editing

I truly believe book editors are what make the entire publishing industry work. Without a properly edited book, your information wouldn't be cohesive or effective in implementing the transformation intended for your readers.

Given how expensive publishing a book can be, I understand all the myriad ways that new authors attempt to cut costs. One way new writers will attempt to do this is by editing their own work. I can assure you this is a monumental mistake, regardless of how great of a writer you may feel you are.

Think about it…In order to do a proper editing job, you need to be able to look at a piece with fresh eyes. This means you would have to effectively forget your *entire* book, which involves waiting at least a year (or two!) before being able to pick up the red pen. I strongly suspect you don't have that kind of time to waste.

I cannot stress this enough: do not rely solely on yourself for editing, and do not try to skimp out on this process. The saying goes that you can't judge a book by its cover, but, as much as we want to believe that won't happen to us, people do judge books by their covers—all day, every day. (I'm even a judge for book award submissions and it's my job to judge books by their covers.)

But while the cover will be the deciding factor in whether someone picks up your book, your editing (or lack thereof) will be the determining factor of whether your reader sticks with your book or not. As a thought leader putting your book into the world, there's no scenario in which you can afford to forgo the editing process. You must be putting the best representation of yourself into the world to attain the goals you've set for yourself and your book. But if you put a book out there that hasn't been reviewed by a professional, you're in serious jeopardy of harming your personal and professional brand.

Self-Editing

Self-editing is exactly as it sounds. It's the process of reviewing your manuscript yourself and editing it yourself, *before* going to a professional editor. This is not to be confused with self-editing *in lieu* of hiring a professional.

The primary reason for doing a thorough self-edit, before working with professional editors, is that when you're paying them for their time to support your book, you want them to be focusing on the areas that matter. Not spending countless time fixing spelling mistakes that a simple spell check could have caught.

If we go back to our previous koi fish analogy, if you don't do a self-edit before hiring a professional, you're basically stopping at the point where your fish is a blob of ice that somewhat resembles the shape of the fish. But there's no clarity on what type of fish it is. When you go through the self-editing process, it'll become clear that you're carving a koi fish, and the collective job for you and the professional editor will then be to make it the best koi fish sculpture possible.

> I truly believe book editors are what make the entire publishing industry work.

Spelling & Grammar Check

You would be shocked at how PYP receives manuscripts from authors looking to publish with us who haven't even performed a spell check on their books. Yes, I know one of the previous writing tips was to turn off spelling and grammar checks, but you must run your manuscript through it before engaging an editor.

Editors are fully capable of focusing on spelling, but wouldn't you prefer they be editing and reviewing for misuses of words rather than obvious errors a computer tool could have picked up? When editors are focused on just your spelling, their minds are not plugged into elevating your manuscript—unless you hire another editor to focus on elevation after you've hired someone to clean up your shitty first draft. But that will cost you more money, and it's money that isn't being spent wisely.

You'll want to run your draft through grammar checks too. This isn't to say that all grammar programs are going to be 100 percent perfect because they won't be, but they'll get your manuscript in better shape for when you're ready to hand it off to professionals.

AI Editing Support

Basic spell checkers and grammar checkers are a form of AI (artificial intelligence) support. But there are other programs such as Grammarly and ProWritingAid that take it to the next level. I've been using Grammarly for years and even have it as a Gmail plugin for all of my emails. Both of these programs are a more sophisticated form that will really help you elevate your writing—again, *before* it gets to a professional editor. Of course, there will be instances when they suggest you do something a certain way and you'll come to find out it isn't correct, but on the whole, they're fairly accurate.

Trusting Your Editor

It may be hard to even think about handing your manuscript off to someone else for review, but at some point you have to let your baby go and visit someone else for a bit. Putting your trust in an editor you don't know and then trusting that they're going to do right by your book can be scary. But know that a good editor is going to do everything they can to elevate your work. They are not being paid by how many redlines they slash through your document. Their goal is to make your work better than they found it.

Trusting an editor can be hard even on small corrections, let alone when they suggest significant changes. We'll cover the different types of editors in just a bit. When I was working on my memoir *House on Fire*[27] I had a handful of pages that went into deep detail on the impact physical running had on me as I was leading up to running a full marathon. My editor made a suggestion to remove nearly all of it. She wanted to keep the climax of the story I was telling—the actual crossing of the finish line of the race—but the backstory leading up to it, she felt, wasn't critical.

This hurt. It was such an important part of my story, but she said, "The section has a fast-paced read to it, then we get to the running part, and it slows the whole story down. Once it's past the story, the speed picks back up again." On hearing her feedback I went back through and tried to read it as if I were my own reader, and I could clearly see what she was saying. She was right. And as a result, I removed multiple pages. The book is better for it. It won't always be easy trusting someone else in this process, but as long as you keep it front and center that an editor is here to make it better, it makes it feel less difficult.

At this point in your writing process, when you're doing this final self-edit before handing your work over to the professionals, I want to acknowledge that you *will* be exhausted with your own words, your book, and yourself. By the time you're doing this self-edit, you'll have read your manuscript at least a dozen times already and you'll start becoming fatigued by it. It's still important to push past that fatigue and give it your all, so that way the next step continues to enhance what you've done. And a word of caution: you'll still have to read your manuscript at least a dozen more times—sorry to be the bearer of bad news (more on that later).

---

27 Jenn T. Grace, *House on Fire* (Hartford, CT: Publish Your Purpose Press, 2020), https://publishyourpurpose.com/authors/jenn-t-grace/.

> If done right, the editing process is collaborative. I often say that publishing is a team sport. While you may have spent a lot of time alone writing your book, the reality is that it takes a team of experienced professionals to bring your book to greatness.

The Four Stages of Editing

If done right, the editing process is collaborative. I often say that publishing is a team sport. While you may have spent a lot of time alone writing your book, the reality is that it takes a team of experienced professionals to bring your book to greatness. While previously discussing self-editing, I used the word *editors* as a collective group, but the reality is that there are multiple types of editing functions with varying skill sets, which many don't realize. We often view editors as the group that fixes punctuation and spelling, but that's just one part of the process.

Being able to distinguish among the four stages is important because any editor you approach with your manuscript will want to know which stage your work is in before sharing their rates and services. Let's take a look at the four stages of non-fiction editing.

1. Developmental Editing

Developmental editing, or structural editing, looks at your story on a macro level, taking into account storyline, structure, and consistency. Anytime you rearrange or delete chapters or rewrite entire blocks of text, you're engaging in developmental editing. This stage takes into account the flow and clarity of your narrative, all with reader engagement in mind.

Because developmental editing is so big-picture (and has the most consequential changes to your draft), it's often the first stage of editing, and it can take anywhere from one to three months or longer.

Not every manuscript will require this level of editing. If your work is in good structural shape, a professional may recommend moving right along to line editing. If you want to have someone looking at it from this vantage point though, even if it doesn't need it, you can absolutely do that. It will only make your work stronger because there will always be an area that has room for improvement.

2. Line Editing

While developmental editing focuses on the big picture, line editing looks at your work on a micro-level. Line editors go paragraph by paragraph and line by line to examine things such as syntax, verbiage, pacing, and flow, ensuring consistency throughout the work. The focus here is less on the story and more on sentence structure, so this type of editing clears up language without changing the storyline. Line editing typically takes one to two months.

Line editing and the next stage, copyediting, are often done together by the same editor. At PYP we combine these two stages.

3. Copyediting

Where line editing is concerned with an author's particular writing style, copyediting is concerned with grammar and ensuring a book follows a particular style guide. Copyediting a full-length book takes about a month.

This is the stage that people are most familiar with. When someone says, "Hey, I can help you edit your book," it's usually someone with copyediting skills. I notice that finding a copy editor can often be the hardest for new authors because so many people believe they have copy editing skills, even if they don't. That's not to say they aren't capable of editing short-form content, such as a blog post or website copy, but copyediting a book requires a more specialized skill.

As you're looking to hire a copy editor for your project, you'll want to make sure you're working with someone with book experience specifically. As much as we love our retired elementary school English teacher or our friend with an English degree, they aren't going to perform the comprehensive-level job that your book requires for you to be taken seriously as a thought leader.

4. Proofreading

Now I'm sure you're thinking, *A fourth stage? Really?!* Trust me: after you've been scouring a draft for months, your eyes start reading what they want to read on the page, not what the actual words are.

Proofreading refers to the detailed correction of a final draft, either just before or just after the layout process. While many eyes have been on your draft up until this point, having that final proof is critical to catch any lingering typos, such as extra spaces or missing punctuation. Proofreading should be the quickest stage, but it can still take two to three weeks depending on the length of the manuscript.

It's not uncommon for your manuscript to have made it through all of these stages of editing, only to still find typos after it has been laid out and you're reviewing a physical or digital proof. As much as that might feel like a kick to the stomach, it's a natural part of the process. When you have a document that's 30,000, 50,000, or 70,000 words, still finding a dozen or so typos at the end of it is par for the course. That's why this process is so rigorous and exhausting.

Battling Exhaustion

At the point where you're copyediting or proofreading, you'll be exhausted from looking at your own work. I promise you that. I'm exhausted from writing this book and it hasn't even started the editing process.

But what I cannot emphasize enough is—now is *not* the time to get sloppy. Now is *not* the time to say, "It's close enough." Now is *not* the time to skim through your editors' corrections or suggestions. When this happens, it will bite you in the butt later. I promise. It's much more difficult to change content when the book has been laid out in its final form to be printed than it is when it's still going back and forth in Word or Google Docs.

At PYP, it sometimes doesn't matter how often we say this or warn our authors of the repercussions of fatigue at this phase, it still happens from time to time. And when it does, it feels devastating. It's a blow to our ego because we see so many typos being caught, and that imposter syndrome creeps back in and says—

I told you you weren't good enough to write a book.
See, you aren't as great as you think you are. You shouldn't have tried this at all.

That voice in our heads comes in really loud and really clear, making us question the entire process. We question ourselves, our abilities, the team we've hired, and the people around us—everything is up for scrutiny. So slow down, take your time, and be thorough. And if you need an extension for your editing timeline, tell your editor or publisher. They can work with you to make sure you're given the right amount of time and space to do this right.

Bottom Line: You Can Do This!

The editing process can be mostly completed prior to working with a publisher, or you can wait until you engage a publisher and begin the process at that time. Publishing houses (the good ones anyway) will have standards for editing quality, so even if you've gone through the editing process first with professionals, there's still a chance that you'll go through the publisher's process too. At the very least you'll be required to go through a proofread, because no publisher will take your manuscript as is without that final set of eyes from their editors first.

Alright, we're to the end of Part 2. This means you have all the right skills and knowledge to construct a strategic and intentional first draft of your manuscript. You've gone from a shitty first draft to a self-edited draft that's now ready for the eyes of a professional editor. Now let's dive into all of the nuances of finding the right publisher and publishing path for you!

> Putting your trust in an editor you don't know and then trusting that they're going to do right by your book can be scary. But know that a good editor is going to do everything they can to elevate your work.

GROW FURTHER

Join the Publish Your Purpose 30-Day Book Writing Challenge to create momentum, access accountability, and get one step closer to a rough first draft by having 30 days of writing tips delivered to your inbox daily.

Access the challenge here:
https://publishyourpurpose.com/30-day-book-writing-challenge/

Did You Catch a Typo?

In this chapter we talked about those pesky typos making their way into your final book, as well as how this can happen and that, when it does, you fix it and keep moving forward.

Did you catch a typo in this book? If so, send me an email at jgrace@publishyourpurpose.com and we'll send you extra bonus content!

PROMOTE YOUR PURPOSE

Find a Book Club

Book clubs are a great opportunity to get in front of an enthusiastic group of readers. Take time to see what book clubs might be a good fit for your book. A great way to learn about book clubs is by asking your friends. See if you know anyone who hosts a book club or is part of a book club and can suggest your book for their upcoming reading.

Don't forget to write these down in the document you previously started to ensure everything is in one easy-to-find place.

PART 3
PUBLISHING

Welcome to Part 3: Publishing. The following chapters are going to help you fully understand the publishing landscape so that you're able to make the most informed decision about what publishing path you'd like to pursue. Additionally, if you're opting to engage with a publisher to get your book into the hands of your readers, this chapter will give you best practices and guidance on how to pick the best publisher for you and your book.

CHAPTER 11
Your Publishing Needs, Wants, and Desires

When we think about who to work with as a publisher, we often aren't thinking about this in a relational type of way. We're conditioned to believe that there's a hierarchy in publishing; that the publisher is this omnipresent being who is here to decide whether your story or work is valuable enough to be published. The reality, though, is that your relationship with your publisher should first be a relationship and not a transaction, but further, it should be equitable. You are the author, and you hold the power to tell your story how you want to tell it.

Before we cover your publishing options in the next chapter, I want to first start by helping you gain a better understanding of what you need, want, or desire from your publisher. This chapter is called "Your Publishing Needs, Wants, and Desires" because I want you to think about what you need in this relationship, not what you'll be provided without your say in the matter.

Too often, we as authors put our entire book's livelihood into the all-knowing, all-seeing, omnipresent publisher. But the reality is, you, if you want it, have so much more control over your relationship with your publisher than you may realize.

Let's take a moment to sit and reflect on this question: What do *you* want from your relationship with your publisher? This might be something you've never really given thought to because you didn't know you could. Often in the publishing industry, there's an inherent hierarchy between authors and publishers. The publisher is put on a pedestal and you, the author, are expected to be enamored by the idea that this publisher has the final say to give your book project the green light/time of day.

The reality is that for many, publishing a book is fulfilling a lifelong dream to become an author. For some of you, this dream has been alive for as long as you can remember. For others, it may be that you've dedicated a significant amount of time to this, so the idea of putting your entire dream of becoming an author into the hands of a publisher can be scary—and—not necessary. And to add to this, predatory publishers know that you're viewing the world through the lens of fulfilling a dream, which leaves you susceptible and vulnerable to being taken advantage of.

You, as an author, have the autonomy to make the publishing decision that's best for you. You are not beholden to the opinion of one person at one publishing house to validate whether your story is worth telling. If you've taken the time to write your story, then it *is* worth telling—you don't need any publishing professional to tell you that. However, this power imbalance between authors and publishers can make you feel like you do need that validation. Additionally, gatekeeping is a very real thing in the publishing industry, meaning a select few at the top are the ones who are deciding whose story is worthy of being heard. This isn't an even or equitable playing field.

I'm here to tell you that your story is good enough, your subject-matter expertise is good enough, and *you* are good enough. You *do not* need the validation of anyone else.

Now, if we can agree that you know your story is worth telling, your book is worth publishing, and you have options, the world is going to open up with available options for you. But in order to know which publishing path and option is going to be best for you, we first need to understand what you need and desire in your relationship with your publisher.

All Publishers Are *Not* Created Equal

If you reflect back to earlier chapters, where we discussed your purpose, your vision, and your goals, we can start to see indicators of what your publishing needs may be and what you desire in a publisher.

Let me first state, very clearly, *all publishers are not created equal*. I cannot emphasize this enough. This is where I spend a fair amount of my time at PYP, educating authors about the fact that all publishers are not created equal.

> Too often, we as authors put our entire book's livelihood into the all-knowing, all-seeing, omnipresent publisher. But the reality is, you, if you want it, have so much more control over your relationship with your publisher than you may realize.

A way to think about this is through the lens of car makes and models. Will a Hyundai from a used car lot and a Bentley from the dealership both have the ability to physically get you from point A to point B? Yes. Will your experience purchasing from a used car dealer and a dealership be different? Also yes. Will your experience driving a used Hyundai versus a brand-new Bentley be different? Yes.

While the mechanics of the process may be the same, such as the ability for us to drive from one place to another or for our books to be published and in the hands of the reader, the path we take to get there is an entirely different scenario/conversation/story. We'll get into the specific nuanced differences in Chapter 14, but here I want to focus on what you need, desire, or want.

Your Wants and Desires

Before continuing, I encourage you to take five minutes to jot down what you want and desire in your relationship with a publisher. Don't overthink it, just write down what comes to you. Use the accompanying workbook to write your answers down (you can download it at www.PublishYourPurpose.com/book-extras.)

Now let's acknowledge that there's a difference between your publishing needs and your wants and desires. Think of this list as "must-have" versus "nice-to-have." Dream big; write it all down.

Let's also acknowledge that every book is different. Every genre is different. Every author's end goals are different. When we look at these differences in their totality, we want to remember not to compare ourselves. Focus on what *you* need, not what someone else has told you that you need. All aspects of the publishing process will vary based on your needs, so really spending the time to figure this out will benefit you in the long run.

I'm going to give you a couple of examples for you to consider when centering in on your search for the best publishing path for you.

YOUR PUBLISHING NEEDS, WANTS, AND DESIRES

What Kind of Relationship with Your Publisher Do You Need, Want, or Desire?

Please note my usage of the word "relationship" in this question. In an ideal world, you'll have a relationship with your publisher. Your publisher is someone who has your back, understands your vision, and will work collaboratively with you to make it happen.

Many publishers operate transactionally; you're just a number on a profit-and-loss statement in their business, just another author running through their process, a cog in a wheel, as it were. This isn't to say that all publishers who operate transactionally are bad. Publishers have different business models, just as a used car dealership and a luxury brand dealership do. This is why it's essential to know what's important to you in this process. If you don't mind being a cog in a wheel and aren't looking for a high-end personal touch experience, there will be plenty of publishers out there for you to work with. You just need to know what you're getting before signing a contract.

The value of having a true relationship with a publisher is that they are there with you for the long haul. They are your partner and the coparent of your book baby. You've collaborated and created this book together, and they are there to support your book throughout its lifetime. When you have a question about your book, can you go to them for an answer? When you notice that your book is suddenly not displaying on your favorite book retailer, will they help you solve the problem? When you have a big opportunity for your book's exposure, do you have someone to brainstorm with to see whether it's the right opportunity for your book? Really think through the long-term goals of your book and try to see whether you want this level of support or you're a DIYer and are fine problem-solving independently.

What I want to avoid for you is a mismatch of expectations. You cannot roll into a used car dealership and expect the experience you'd get purchasing a Bentley. Nor can you expect the wow factor to be the same for a used Hyundai versus a new Bentley. It just doesn't work that way. So look inward to think, *Am I looking for a long-term partnership with a publisher, or am I looking for a vendor or service provider to get the job done?*

Wherever you land in this spectrum is great, with no judgment. You just want to make sure you know what you're getting so that when you start asking and/or demanding a level of service, you're working with the right publisher who will be able to deliver on it, in a way that you expect and are pleased with.

What Level of Collaboration Will You Need, Want, or Desire in the Process?

As people, we enter any new environment with default settings of who we are and what we expect. The next question for you to consider is what level of collaboration you need. Personally, I'm a super collaborative person. This book is a great example of that. I sought input and advice from many different people to ensure I was constructing this book in the best way possible. Others might arrive at this same level and quality of book without collaborating with anyone along the way. Wherever you land is what works for you.

The benefit of collaboration throughout the publishing process is that when you're working with a publisher who has your best interest in mind, your ability to leverage and amplify your message will significantly increase. You may feel you have everything you need in place, including the right support system, the right resources, and the right vendors, and therefore you may realize you don't need anyone to collaborate with and can go off and independently self-publish—and that's great too. But do you desire a level of collaboration that will make you feel fully supported in the process when the inevitable ups and downs come creeping in?

Collaboration and control can also go hand-in-hand. When you're working with a publisher who isn't collaborative, oftentimes they are in control and are in the driver's seat, which means they're making important decisions that could have a ripple effect of impacts on the long-term success of your book. If you have the knowledge of knowing what you want your distribution strategy to be, for example, you'll need to strongly advocate for yourself in the absence of a collaborative partner. But knowing what you and your book need at the most intimate level of detail will be *your* responsibility.

In future chapters, we'll continue evaluating the pros and cons by publishing path.

How Important Is It to You That Your Values Align with Your Publisher's?

Values alignment may be one of the most important considerations in this entire process. You can publish a book whether you're working transactionally or in a relationship. You can publish a book whether your publisher is super collaborative or not collaborative at all. But the question is, how will you feel publishing your book with a publisher who isn't aligned with your values as a person? This may not be an issue for you and, in that case, feel free to move on to the next section. But if this is something you've thought about, I encourage you to keep reading.

If we think about any major decision in life, how important is it to you that you're collaborating with like-minded people or organizations? You can think of this in many ways—whether it's based on a shared interest, geography, politics, or otherwise. Really take a moment to think about where you want to channel your time, energy, money, and other resources. Let's break down a few ways to think about our values.

Corporations vs. Small Businesses

What is your preference on the whole regarding corporations versus small businesses? Are you someone who likes to support corporations such as big banks, big-box retailers, grocery store chains, and chain restaurants? Or do you prefer to support local businesses when possible, such as using a local bank or credit union, supporting your local businesses on Main Street, or supporting the new local restaurant in town?

What many authors don't take into consideration is that traditional publishers are corporations. They are multi-billion-dollar companies, many of which are headquartered in New York City, and they are run with the bottom line in mind first, above all else.

Independent publishers and hybrid publishers alike, however, are the equivalent of supporting your local business. They are smaller, community-minded, and often center their authors in a different way than a corporation might.

In a corporate publishing environment, you may be one of 3,000 authors being published in a season, whereas in an independent or hybrid environment, you might be one of 500, 200, or even 50. A publisher's level of authors being served at any one time may serve as an indicator of how intimate your experience may be with the team supporting you. There are also other variables that we'll get into in future chapters regarding access to traditional publishing versus independent or hybrid publishers.

Personal Values

Are you someone who believes in diversity and inclusiveness and that everyone should have equal access to opportunities? If so, find a publisher who shares those values.

Do you believe that our environment is in crisis, or do you believe that climate change isn't real? Find a publisher who's handling their impact on the environment in different ways depending on what your personal values are.

If you believe that publishing should only be accessible to the elite—people with a certain level of power, authority, or financial means—find a publisher who shares those values.

Are you a politically minded or politically oriented person? If so, find a publisher who shares whatever your political beliefs are.

Whatever your personal values are, find a publisher who shares those values. Make sure to do your homework and your research to ensure you're working with someone who shares those values. There's nothing more disenchanting than signing a contract only to find out within the first few meetings that you've made a big mistake because the publisher you're working with is in opposition to something that is core to who you are as a person or are publishing books that are in complete opposition to your personal beliefs and values. This is a really important step, not to be skipped.

Representation

Representation matters for all individual identities, and the level of importance this plays for you personally is your decision.

- Do you see yourself represented among the authors the publisher has previously published?
- Do you see yourself represented among the publishing house's team?
- Are you female-identified and desire to work with a team that includes women?
- Are you an LGBTQ+ person and desire a team that understands that aspect of who you are?
- Are you a person of color who desires to work with a team that understands, values, and respects your unique perspective?
- Are you a male-identified and desire to work with a diverse team of people?

At PYP, we strongly believe that representation matters. Our mission statement is to elevate the voices often excluded from traditional publishing by intentionally seeking out authors and storytellers with diverse backgrounds, life experiences, and unique perspectives that will make an impact in the world. We believe in free speech and the ability to walk down the street without harassment or persecution. As a hybrid publisher, we wear our mission and values on our sleeves proudly so that we ensure we're working with authors who also share those values.

Bottom Line: You Can Do This!

The bottom line is to not rush this process. Do your homework and due diligence so that you find the fairest and most equitable arrangement that works for *you*.

GROW FURTHER

Watch the *Publish Your Purpose Pick Your Path to Publishing Webinar* to go deeper and gain better clarity on your needs, wants, and desires for your publishing relationship.

Access the webinar here:
https://publishyourpurpose.com/path-publishing-webinar/.

PROMOTE YOUR PURPOSE

Document Your Journey

Even if you know a lot of people who have written books, there are many people who don't know a single person who has. Sharing your experience allows people to be a fly on the wall to your writing process. This will help you with accountability, it'll bring your potential readers along on the ride with you, and it'll help you document your journey for your own posterity.

Don't underestimate the excitement level of those around you who will be telling everyone that someone they know has written a book. Engage with them now and speak to their curiosity by sharing your experience in doing this.

Author Beware— Scams

CHAPTER 12

This chapter is going to continue to go into the evaluation of your publishing needs, but from a different perspective. In this chapter, we're going to cover some of the areas that you should be extra cautious around to ensure that you aren't finding yourself in a publishing situation that's absolutely not the right fit for you.

Publishing Paths

First, it's important to know what your publishing options are. There are three primary paths to getting your book published and into the world. We'll also discuss another type of publisher you'll want to steer clear of at all costs. Let's high-level define the three primary publishing paths.

TRADITIONAL	A publishing house that buys the rights to your book, publishes and sells it, but offers you limited royalties on sales. You are responsible for marketing and book launch efforts.
SELF-PUBLISH	You pay for and manage the publishing process, from editing to printing to marketing—and everything in between.
HYBRID	The publisher manages and guides the process, while you cover the costs, retain creative control, and receive more royalties. The services vary by publisher but include everything from content editing to book launch marketing.

Time vs. Money

Now let's talk about one of the most important decision-making factors for the publishing process, which is honestly a huge determination for many decisions in life: time versus money. The old adage asks, *Do you have more time, or do you have more money?* When it comes to publishing, this is certainly something that will have a big impact on which publishing path you'll choose. There are other variables after you've made this decision that will have a big impact on your ability to pursue your desired path as well, which we'll cover in more detail later.

More Time vs. Money, Scenario 1, Traditional Publishing

If you have more time than money, you could explore a traditional publishing deal. Traditional publishing deals are very difficult to come by, as they require you to have a large platform of followers and a literary agent representing you, among a host of other things. (Sidebar: a literary agent is a person who liaises between an author with a written manuscript and the potential publishers who may be interested in turning it into a book.) A traditional book deal can take you years to acquire, if ever, and once you have a deal, the publishing timeline can be 18–36 months, depending. This can make your total timeline easily three to five years.

If you're looking to speed into the market and it's really important that your book is in the hands of your readers in a shortened time frame, traditional publishing is likely not the right path for you. Remember, they are a corporation and you are one of *many* authors, so there's a much bigger system and structure in place that you, as an author, must move through.

More Time vs. Money, Scenario 2, Self-Publishing

Once again, if you have more time versus money, you may want to explore a self-publishing route. With self-publishing, you have the ability to figure out the publishing process on your own and get your book published in a very short period of time.

There are a number of areas to pay attention to when deciding to go the self-publishing route. The first is that you need to be a really organized person and have good project management skills. If that isn't natural to you, I would consider the next option of hybrid publishing.

When done right, self-publishing can create an incredible quality book. However, many people don't approach it the right way. Since you've been working on your book for so long and it's been percolating in your mind, when you're finally done writing the manuscript, there's this sudden urgency to get it published immediately. I've seen people who've been writing their book for 10 years and once it's done they want to publish it within 60 days. This is hands down the biggest mistake I see self-publishing authors make. The publishing process is not the time to make up for a previously busted timeline; it's not the time to rush.

The two big boulders of the publishing process most authors take into consideration are the cover design and the editing process. Without a strong cover and a properly edited book, nothing else will matter. But beyond those two primary pieces, there are dozens and dozens of micro-decisions that will have a big impact on the success of your book. This is where self-publishing can get tricky because it can be difficult to find a source of information that you trust and that doesn't conflict with 12 other articles you just read about how to pick the right categories for your book to be in. This is where a lot of time will go—researching, digesting, understanding the dozens of steps involved, and then deciding how you want to approach it.

You can absolutely publish a book within 60 days, but I can assure you you'll be sacrificing quality somewhere. Whether it's editing, typesetting (how the book looks on the inside), or the many strategic pieces and parts that really help a book sell, you'll miss something if you're trying to get your book out this quickly.

So, if you have more time, are willing to learn what makes a good book sell, and are able to be patient in getting your book published, self-publishing can be a great path for you. And when I say wait to get it self-published, I mean you can get a really strong book published within six months—so this isn't the three-to-five-year timeline of traditional publishing, but it's also not the 60-day timeline that many "book gurus" suggest.

> The publishing process is not the time to make up for a previously busted timeline; it's not the time to rush.

Your book is a part of you. It's a part of your identity. Once it's in the world you cannot take it back; once it's out, it's out. If you want to make a good first impression, you must follow industry best practices. Otherwise, all of the benefits you're trying to gain by publishing a book will be negated when you aren't being taken seriously because your book looks amateur.

This is where the goals we outlined earlier come into play. If you're looking to position yourself as a thought leader, seeking colleges or universities that will adopt your book as part of course curriculum, or seeing your book on the shelf of a bookstore, you *must* follow best practices because a poorly created self-published book will not get you to those end goals.

To wrap this up, let me say that I'm a big believer in self-publishing, just please slow down, take your time, and do it in alignment with best practices. This will help you achieve the success that you're looking for.

More Money vs. Time, Scenario 3, Hybrid Publishing

If you find yourself with more money than time, hybrid publishing is potentially a good route for you. I often describe hybrid publishing as the best of both worlds.

I first want to note that with traditional publishing, it's often believed that you don't have to pay any expenses for the publishing of your book, but that's a myth (more on this in Chapter 16.) There are costs no matter how you publish your book, it's just a matter of what you're paying for and what you're getting in return for that payment.

With hybrid publishing, you're investing your money into the publishing process, but you're getting a team of dedicated industry professionals helping you navigate the process, which avoids that steep learning curve that self-publishing often creates. And there are times when self-publishing costs more in the long run simply because of not knowing what you don't know, such as following a process out of order that causes you to have to repeat it—and that can cost you more money.

A hybrid publisher is an independent publishing service that combines the professional expertise of a traditional publishing house with the high profitability of self-publishing. Every hybrid publisher is different and has a different business model, so it's important to find the right hybrid publisher that works for you. Some hybrids have a low upfront fee and take higher royalties, and some have a high upfront fee and take lower royalties (We'll discuss royalties in further detail in Chapter 14.) Fees can range from $5,000 to $100,000 or more. This is why having the right information to find the right publisher for you is imperative, which we'll go over in more detail in just a moment.

Are Hybrid Publishers Legitimate?

If you're knee-deep in publishing house research, you might've seen some not-so-great reviews of hybrid publishers. There are a number of potential reasons for this, one of them being that the hybrid publisher was low-quality. It's not against the law to be a mediocre hybrid publisher, so it's up to you to vet your potential publishers to find the most reputable one for your book. Another reason could be that the hybrid publisher was a vanity press in disguise. This happens more often than you'd expect because vanity presses are designed to trick you.

Vanity Publishers

What this chapter is teeing us up for is what to beware of in the publishing industry. Unfortunately, because there's a lack of information, it can be hard to discern the difference between a vanity publisher and a hybrid publisher. If you're evaluating the path of hybrid publishing, then this is information you need to know.

A vanity publisher, a.k.a. vanity press, is a scam publishing scheme that takes your money and produces a low-quality, throw-away book. Sneaky vanity publishers are skilled at disguising themselves as hybrid publishers. Because, let's face it, it's not in their interest to say, "Hey! We're a vanity press and here to scam you!" This can make it super confusing for authors to differentiate between scams and reputable publishing opportunities.

How To Spot a Vanity Publisher vs. a Hybrid Publisher

If reputable hybrid publishers and scam vanity publishers are both claiming to be professional, worthwhile publishing investments, how can we spot the difference? The business models for hybrid publishers and vanity publishers seem similar on the surface. In both models, authors pay the publishing house to publish their books. The difference is that vanity publishers are focused only on making money (sometimes from the authors themselves!), while hybrid publishers actually care about the books they publish and the success of their authors.

A Hybrid Publisher Will:

- Be certified by the Independent Book Publishers Association (IBPA)
- Have a vested interest in producing a high-quality book
- Provide quality distribution and marketing services
- Have quality publication standards
- Foster professional author–publisher relationships
- Are transparent around publishing costs and fees
- Not meet the above stated requirements!

Consider the Following Questions When Researching and Reviewing Publishers

1. Are They Certified by the IBPA?

The best indicator that a hybrid publisher is legitimate is whether it's approved by the IBPA, the gold standard for reputable hybrid publishers that follows strict best practices and quality-control requirements.

2. Do They Produce High-Quality Books?

Quality is everything in publishing. Without it having high-quality writing, editing, and design, few people will read your book. If you're a thought leader and want your book to help accelerate your career, it's even more important.

When vetting a prospective publisher, it's important to research books that the publisher has released. Ask yourself whether the quality meets industry standards (and your personal standards). While many hybrid publishers can meet and exceed industry quality standards, most vanity publishers fall short. This is an easy way to distinguish between the two.

3. Do They Have a Vested Interest in Producing a High-Quality Book?

Looking into the business model of the publisher in question can also help indicate whether they will produce a high-quality book. Vanity publishers operate differently than hybrid publishers. Often, a vanity publisher will offer 100 percent of royalties to authors. While this may seem like a great opportunity, the reality is often grimmer. Because vanity publishers receive 0 percent in royalties, they often contractually require authors to buy thousands of copies of their own books, even if they are using a print-on-demand model. Rather than profiting off the book, the vanity publisher profits from the authors directly. If there's no incentive to actually sell the book to readers, there's no real incentive for the publisher to produce a high-quality book. Remember: just because you're paying top dollar doesn't mean you're getting professional quality.

4. Do They Have Quality Publication Standards?

A vanity press will publish virtually any book, as long as the author pays. Hybrid publishers have a quality review process in which they only accept books that meet internal requirements. For example, PYP, which is a hybrid publisher, focuses on high-quality non-fiction books and memoirs related to social change. A good way to check the quality of the books by the publisher in question is to look up some books by the publisher or talk to previous authors directly. Check to see whether any of the books have made it to bestseller lists or have won any awards. Read reviews or watch testimonials from other authors to survey their experiences.

> Your book is a part of you. It's a part of your identity. Once it's in the world you cannot take it back; once it's out, it's out.

5. Do They Provide Quality Marketing and Distribution?

A reputable hybrid publisher is responsible for the distribution of your book, including offering printing and fulfillment services. PYP goes above and beyond, helping the author design a unique marketing plan that fits their goals, and then helping them implement it. A vanity press typically publishes through Amazon's Kindle Direct Publishing (KDP) platform. While this works for some books, it provides a large accessibility obstacle if the author wants bookstores, retailers, libraries, and universities to access the book. Amazon's business model includes keeping business on Amazon, so they have no incentive to make their books appealing to other retailers. As a reminder, vanity publishers make money from selling books to authors and do not have a vested interest in helping the author make their book easily accessible to non-Amazon booksellers.

6. Do They Foster Professional Author–Publisher Relationships?

A hybrid publisher has professional coaching, editing, design, and publishing teams to guide you through the publishing process. They will take the time to foster a strong, professional relationship with authors. Authors should feel supported and like they have a say in the creative process. A vanity press, in contrast, might be difficult to reach and disconnected from the author and the author's experience. Many vanity publishers use automated customer service software to answer author questions. With communication barriers like that, authors can feel disconnected from and unsupported in the publishing process. In many cases, vanity presses own the full rights to the books they publish. This means that to save time and energy, they might not even consult the author over items such as book formatting, cover design, and writing style—and there's nothing authors can do about it contractually.

7. Are They Transparent about Publishing Costs and Fees?

A sign that you're working with a vanity publisher and not a hybrid publisher comes down to the transparency of costs and fees of publishing.

If the publisher is unable to give you a thorough breakdown of how and where your money is being spent, it's likely that they're cushioning the costs and pocketing the difference. A quality hybrid publisher will be able to tell you exactly how much money it will cost to cover editing, design, distribution, and every part of the publishing process. Hybrid publishers will not add on additional fees or book purchase requirements, so that's a good sign that you're not operating with a vanity press.

Bottom Line: You Can Do This!

The bottom line is to be aware of what you're getting yourself into if you choose the path to hire support to get your book published.

A resource I mention on a regular basis is the Alliance of Independent Authors (ALLi)Watchdog List.[28] This list monitors the independent publishing industry, acting as a whistleblower for publishers that exploit authors. If you have a sense that something isn't adding up with the publisher you're talking to, if they have shady practices, then you'll find them here.

---

28 https://www.allianceindependentauthors.org/watchdog/

GROW FURTHER

Protect yourself in the publishing industry by downloading the 9 Questions to Ask a Publisher blueprint so that you know the right questions to ask to ensure you won't be scammed.

Access the blueprint here:
https://publishyourpurpose.com/questions-ask-publisher/.

PROMOTE YOUR PURPOSE

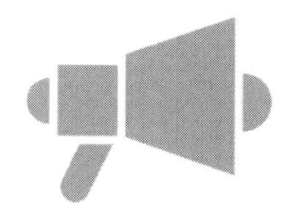

Test Drive Your Content

A beautiful byproduct of writing a book is that you have a ton of content and a lot of time to get it just right. A great way to engage with your potential readers is by test-driving your content. Post your content in a LinkedIn post, on your blog or website, or in your newsletter. Tell your readers that this will be part of your book and that you're looking for feedback. This gives them an opportunity to engage with you and your content and get excited about the fact that you have a forthcoming book.

CHAPTER 13
Author Beware— Censorship

In addition to the fact that there are simply more scam publishing companies in the industry than you can shake a stick at, there are also more subtle areas to keep an eye out for.

Censorship has been an issue for as long as humans have been on this earth, and it's your job as the author to ensure you're protecting your voice— and depending on who you are, the odds may be stacked against you.

Protecting Your Story in the Publishing Industry

One of the most beautiful things about the publishing industry is that every author brings a unique story to the table. Publishing a book has the magical quality of bringing a person's experiences and lessons to life, on paper, in a way that allows them to share their distinctive perspective on the world with their readers. One author's voice has the power to bring unprecedented clarity and insights to their audience in a way that no other author can.

Unfortunately, as much as the publishing industry is an avenue that gives writers a platform to share their unique voices, it's also a system that has taken away and repressed the voices of others. Like nearly all major industries, the world of publishing has, in part, been shaped by deep institutional and structural racism and bias against underrepresented communities.

Leadership in the big US-based publishing houses has historically been composed of predominantly white cisgender straight men, and the majority of editors in these houses have been white cisgender straight women.

With so little diversity in the roles that have a large influence over the editing and production of books, sometimes books from underrepresented authors can be inadvertently or purposefully changed to match that specific perspective.

There are already high barriers for underrepresented authors to cross to make it into the big publishing houses, but oftentimes the editing process is an unforeseen obstacle in itself. In order to sell a book to their audience, the larger publishing houses may use their influence in the editing process to heavily alter the message or writing style/unique voice of their diverse authors. And to cater to their specific audience, these editors might comb through authors' works and remove key details that reveal their background (gender, ethnicity, sexual orientation, religious beliefs, age, etc.). In taking away an author's identity, editors are taking away the unique experiences that have shaped and changed the author's voice; they are, in essence, taking the author out of the book.

Harmful Repercussions

Having an editor or publisher drastically change your book may lead to a disconnect between you and your audience. For example, if your target demographic is Gen Z students just entering college, you might have certain words or pop culture references embedded in your book, specifically to connect with a younger generation. However, if your publisher wants to market your book to an older age group that's the primary buyer of their books, they might change or remove the references and terms you've chosen to include. This may make your book more "sellable" to a larger range of readers, but you'll lose that extra touch of relatability that would've made your book 10 times more meaningful to the group you originally wrote the book for.

Also, if you're using your book as a way to market yourself to potential clients or future employers, a heavily edited book may significantly impact that opportunity upon arrival. If your book fits into a standard mold that anyone could've written, then people will be less moved to interact with you further. However, if your book is full of your heart and you're constantly drawing readers in with your story, then people will already know how amazing you are and take that next step to reach out. You and your book should match, so don't let editors take away your relationship with your audience and your future clients.

If one of your goals for writing your book is to provide representation for your audience and readers, it's really important that your book sustains that quality through the editing process. Sometimes the smallest details in the stories you write will hold deep meaning for your readers. Representation can be a very healing and empowering thing for people who may have felt alone or unseen. Editors may inadvertently or purposefully take out those little rare gems of representation that are sprinkled throughout the pages of your book if they feel as though they are insignificant or don't match their desired style. Remember that you're not only giving yourself strength through writing a book, but you're also helping countless readers. So fight for your readers and their stories when you're faced with a challenging editing process.

How Editors Censor Your Words

We all know the importance of editing when it comes to getting published, but what that editing looks like will vary depending on the publisher you choose. You may get back a manuscript that doesn't at all resemble what you submitted in the first place. Even worse, you may feel like the publishing house completely edited out your voice and message altogether. Here's how and why publishing house editors may censor your work.

Why Publishing House Editors Change Your Content

In order to understand why publishing house editors change your content, let's take a look at the traditional publishing house process.

Traditional publishers invest heavily in you at the beginning of the publishing process, giving you an advance, hiring all the necessary editors (plural!), and handling some of the marketing and promotion of your book (although more often than not, you'll have to use money from your advance toward public relations efforts). With all these upfront costs, traditional publishers have a vested financial interest in making sure your book sells enough copies to cover both the costs of publishing *and* turn a profit for themselves. Meeting those goals means editing and making changes to your book so it can best appeal to its audience base.

Regardless of the target audience you had in mind while you were writing your book, your publisher and their marketing team may alter your work to better market it to their audience.

How Publishing House Editors Censor Your Work

What do these changes and edits look like? All non-fiction editing involves small incremental changes such as swapping out words, removing redundancies, and adding content here and there. That's standard procedure to make sure your work is the best it can possibly be.

Censoring comes into play when publishing house editors deliberately remove or change the content in order to cater to the audience they're selling to. Censoring can come in many forms. The important thing is recognizing when censorship is happening and knowing what rights you have in place that would allow you to do something about it.

CASE STUDY #1 FROM PYP ARCHIVES

A Black female author tried to submit an article to an online journal. When she got back her revised work, the editor had removed any cultural references directly related to the Black community. This was done intentionally to neutralize the article for the journal's target audience.

CASE STUDY #2 FROM PYP ARCHIVES

An author pitched his memoir to a traditional publishing house. The publishing house editors came back with a proposal: the main character should be gay. It didn't matter that the author of the memoir wasn't gay; the publisher was tailoring the story to meet its audience and attempting to appropriate LGBTQ+ experiences for a more "salacious" narrative.

> One author's voice has the power to bring unprecedented clarity and insights to their audience in a way that no other author can.

Which Types of Publishers Might Censor Your Work?

The type of editorial control you have will depend on the type of publisher you go with.

Traditional Publishing Houses
Traditional publishers handle all of the publishing and *some* of the marketing for you. Because they're paying you upfront in the form of an advance (the industry average is $2,500), they're also most likely to censor and alter your work to ensure it is well-received by their target audience.

Self-Publishing
Since you're the one who's making all the decisions about your book, you retain full control over who edits and designs it. You're also the one making the marketing decisions and are able to market specifically to your target audience.

Hybrid Publishing
Hybrid publishers will work with you through the publishing process, giving you the resources and team that you need in order to have your book published. The editing process with hybrid publishers is more collaborative because they have your best interest at heart, not how much money they can make off you.

Choosing an Editor

One of the best ways to ensure that your authentic writing style and voice will be protected is by selecting the right editor to read your work. A good way of knowing right off the bat whether an editor is the right one for you is if you feel like you can also give them feedback. Sometimes it might feel like you shouldn't push back against what an editor is suggesting because you're hiring them to point out the weaknesses you may have been too close to the work to see, but that isn't the case. You're the person who best knows the heart and purpose of your book, and you should defend it if someone tries to alter the central message too greatly. An editor should be a person you can have an open dialogue with about any of the changes they recommend. When choosing an editor, you should pick a person who feels approachable; someone you'd feel comfortable with raising your concerns about protecting your voice.

You should also choose an editor who you can trust. Sometimes this means working with an editor you already know or a friend who has experience and training in editing your specific genre of book, but it doesn't always have to be the case. You can develop a good relationship with an editor even if you start off as strangers. The most important thing you can do to determine whether you can trust the editor you're considering is to have a conversation with them. Enter the relationship by outlining what you want to gain from publishing your book and what kind of impact you want your particular story to have. Share with them your intentions behind your narrative style and what kind of readers you're hoping to reach with your work. If they're excited by your ideas and demonstrate a sincere interest in delivering your imagined product to your readers, then they could be the right editor to work with.

Another thing to consider when picking an editor is looking for someone with a similar background (gender, ethnicity, sexual orientation, religious beliefs, age, etc.) to you or your audience. You can definitely have an amazing editing experience with an editor who's completely different from you, but if you're really concerned about having your unique voice edited away or flattened, this is a great option. Someone who shares your background might be more likely to recognize the importance of adding certain terms or colloquialisms to your work, as well as certain spellings or writing styles, while others might want to edit them out or change them. Having an editor who shares the same background as your audience will also give them more incentive to protect what you're trying to do because they know the benefit and value of your work and will want to make sure others receive that same gift.

> You and your book should match, so don't let editors take away your relationship with your audience and your future clients.

Avoiding Censorship: PYP's Approach to Editing

When I had the inklings of starting PYP in 2014 and 2015, I was supporting a friend through writing and publishing her first book. At this point, I had already self-published three books of my own, so I was someone she trusted to navigate this journey with her. She had hired a reputable hybrid publisher and, on the whole, her book came out phenomenal. However, the fiasco of the editing process is where things took a bit of a detour—and from this experience, I vowed that if I ever started a publishing company I would *not* do it this way.

The editing process started off harmless for her. She was paired with an editor but in a very unintentional type of way. She was a new author and the publisher had an editor available, so only because of timing were the two forced to work together. There was no consideration given to personality fit or content interest.

What we learned *very* quickly was that this editor was bringing an overt bias to the table. Her fundamental belief system was in opposition to the very topic my friend was writing about, and this created friction immediately. When we began to review the editing suggestions, it was clear and evident that this editor did not believe in the premise of the book; in fact, she believed the opposite. This level of mismatch caused a lot of problems that could've been avoided.

I politely called the publisher to advise them of the situation. They told me that there was nothing they could do, that was their process, and that was the editor they had available. We tried making it work, but again, the friction bubbled up. I contacted them again. After numerous attempts and an increasing level of demand (and frustration), I was able to get them to provide us with another editor to finish the job.

The challenge with all of this is that if the publisher had taken even a basic consideration of the topics the editors were working on, then my friend could've been spared a lot of emotional duress. This editor questioned every fabric of her being, everything she had been working on for 15 years in her business and had put into the form of her book as a thought leader. She challenged my friend at her core, which shook my friend's foundation as an author and impacted the rest of the process. (And for the record, my friend was writing about the positive impacts of feeling included in the workplace, so this was not a polarizing topic in any way).

As a result of the disconnect I witnessed in this process, I vowed that if I started a publishing company (which had already been on my mind), I would never put any author (or editor) in a situation like this. As a result, our editing process at PYP has taken a completely different approach, which we feel should be an industry standard.

Here are some of the markers of a good editing environment:

1. **Our Editors Have Good Bedside Manner**

    When it comes to good editing, honesty is important—and kindness should be, too! At PYP, we're extremely selective about the editors we choose to work with. Not only do we take actual editing experience into account, but we also look at integrity. Our thorough vetting process has produced an exclusive, curated collective of editors who are really good at what they do—editors who will get you and give constructive feedback. So you can rest assured that if an editor is on our team, they are the real deal—and you won't have to defend the premise of your book like my friend had to.

2. **Our "Editor Matchmaking" Pairs You with the Perfect Editor**

    Once an author decides to work with PYP, what's the first thing we do? Go fish! We send their manuscript in its current form to our team of editors to see who bites. Editors interested in working on it will respond within the week with their preliminary feedback, including what type(s) of editing your manuscript needs (more on this in Chapter 10), how long they need to edit the piece, and why they want to work with you.

    Not only does our "editor matchmaking" process allow us to provide a more accurate price estimate right off the bat, but it also guarantees that whomever you're matched with is someone who understands what you're about and wants to be part of your work.

3. **You Have Veto Power**

   Unlike traditional publishers who alter your work to suit their bottom line, PYP gives you full veto power. This means after we share our editors' preliminary feedback with you, you get to decide which editor to go with. Maybe you want an editor who knows your specialty; maybe you don't. Maybe you don't feel like making one more decision and you say, "You tell me. You're the experts!" Either way, it's your choice.

   If we do push back on one of your decisions (usually when our non-fiction editing expertise tells us something may not be a good strategy), you still have veto power. In this line of work, there are very few non-negotiables—and we'll always explain to you what those are!

Your Story. Your Choice.

As an independent, hybrid publisher, PYP puts our writers first. Not only do we work exclusively with purpose-driven authors who want to make an impact in their communities, we also let you take the lead. Your story is told the way you want it to be.

Bottom Line: You Can Do This!

As much as this chapter is a cautionary tale to help prevent future authors from facing these prevalent biases, we also want to use it as an opportunity to celebrate every author's originality and distinctive story. Your book is a piece of who you are, and no person is invalid or unworthy of being seen or heard. You should be endlessly proud of what you've accomplished in writing a book because not everyone can do that. So, stand by your book and stand up for yourself. You deserve to see the impact that you and your authentic book have on your intended audience.

GROW FURTHER

Protect yourself in the publishing industry by downloading the 9 Questions to Ask a Publisher blueprint so that you know the right questions to ask to avoid censorship in your process.

Access the blueprint here:
https://publishyourpurpose.com/questions-ask-publisher/.

PROMOTE YOUR PURPOSE

Update LinkedIn

Even if you're lacking clarity at this phase, push yourself out of your comfort zone and update your LinkedIn profile to include that you're soon to be a published author. LinkedIn has the option to add a publication where you can include your book's title, subtitle, and description.

This may feel like you're putting the cart well before the horse, but this is about how to promote your book once it's published, even if you're using placeholder information while you develop more clarity. This won't be perfect, not even close, but it'll get you into more conversations about your forthcoming book.

CHAPTER 14
Picking the Best Publishing Path for You

Deciding which publishing path you'll take is one of the most important parts of this process. By now you've seen some of the pros and cons of your three publishing options: traditional publishing, self-publishing, and hybrid publishing. Now we'll go into detail on how to evaluate the best publishing option for you. Regardless of what path you pursue, one thing that every author needs is a Publishing Strategist.

The next time you're perusing your local bookstore, consider this: each of the novels you see before you were labors of love. We're not just referring to the labor of one brilliant writer. Behind every published author is a team of experts who supported and pushed that author through book completion, the publishing finish line, and the post-publishing world. While each role on that team of experts is essential, here's why a good Publishing Strategist can make or break your publishing experience.

What Does a Publishing Strategist Do?

The publishing process has many moving parts, both strategic (like crafting the perfect book description and author bio) and logistic (like getting ISBNs and copyright protection). Your Publishing Strategist is the person who keeps track of those parts to make sure things keep progressing in the right direction—including you!

The person who fills this role doesn't necessarily need to have "Publishing Strategist" in their title or background. But you'll want someone with solid project management experience, preferably someone with experience as a writing or publishing coach.

> When it comes to non-fiction writing, your book is your brand.

It's All About Building Your Brand

When it comes to non-fiction writing, your book is your brand. In order for your book to have the most success, your book, professional brand, and personal brand should all be strategically aligned. A good Publishing Strategist will know how to set your entire business up for success, not just the book. (After all, the book is just a stepping stone!)

Five Key Functions of a Publishing Strategist

Your Publishing Strategist serves five key functions—

1. **Prevent Overwhelm**

    Talk about information overload! One of the hardest parts of publishing is not knowing what you need to do and when you need to do it. This can make it very difficult to stay on track. Your Publishing Strategist is there to lay out a concrete plan for you to follow. That plan could be daily, weekly, or monthly, but the important thing is that it's tailored to whatever is realistic for you based on how you operate best.

2. **Hold You Accountable**

    Your Publishing Strategist holds you accountable for the timeline you worked so hard to establish together. This includes making sure you're meeting deadlines and accounting for things that might prevent you from meeting those deadlines, such as ensuring you're staying on topic as you finish your book.

3. **Provide Marketing Guidance**

    When you're in the middle of finishing a manuscript, it can be hard to focus on anything else. The reality is that you should be marketing your book to your target audience from day one. Not to mention, non-fiction writing requires industry-specific PR and marketing guidance for things like your book launch. Your Publishing Strategist will help you navigate the overwhelming and confusing landscape of book marketing to ensure your book gets off the ground and into the hands of your target audience.

4. **Ensure You Have a Plan After Publishing**

   The work doesn't stop once you're published. Then comes equally important steps, including creating online courses, webinars, and workbooks to complement your book—or even featuring your book on audience-specific podcasts. These should all be part of the post-publication portion of your marketing plan, which your Publishing Strategist can help you navigate.

5. **Share Your Vision and Excitement**

   Your Publishing Strategist should absolutely share your vision and values. That way, you know every decision they're helping you make is with your message in mind. They're also the perfect person to celebrate with once it's all said and done. (After all, who else really knows your struggle if not your Publishing Strategist?!)

Save Yourself Time and Money

Just like investing in an editor is crucial to the success of your book, having a good Publishing Strategist can make or break your publishing experience. Not only do Publishing Strategists help things go more smoothly, but they actually save you money in the long run by helping you get crystal clear on the intent and purpose of your book. This means knowing who your audience is and the best way to reach that audience. It also means knowing how your book will fit into your business and how you can leverage your book to elevate your business.

Authors who are able to answer these questions end up saving time and money in the publishing process because their work often requires less editing. It's also better for your brand, heralding the success of your next book, and your creative well-being.

Trust the process. Publishing a book is an emotional rollercoaster. You'll have days when you question everything. You may even find yourself wondering, *Is this really worth it?* The answer to this question is, yes!

Publishing a book is about more than just bragging rights. There are tangible ways that being a published author can elevate your brand, business, and career trajectory. By having a robust plan in place and the right experts in your corner, you'll be able to trust the process even on rough days.

Discover Your Assets as an Author

As you're deciding which publishing path is going to be best for you and your goals, there's going to be a big elephant in the room: the majority of authors pursuing a traditional publishing deal won't actually have access to that opportunity. This means that if you cannot get a traditional deal, you're really deciding between self-publishing and hybrid publishing.

Let's talk about what a traditional publisher is looking for before we go into key questions to ask your prospective publisher or service provider.

In traditional publishing, everything is a numbers game. As we discussed previously, traditional publishing is a corporate-run environment with a focus on profitability and bottom-line returns to the company. As a result, their focus is on publishing books that will make them a return on that investment.

Audience Size

Traditional publishers are looking for a safe bet—someone they can put their energy and support behind who's going to sell *a lot* of books. A bigger example of this is the release of Prince Harry's memoir *Spare* (January 2023). His book had record-breaking sales of 1.43 million English-language copies on the first day. Penguin Random House (PRH), who published it, paid him a $20 million advance on sales. For PRH to break even on that advance, it expected that 1.7 million copies needed to be sold.[29]

Publishing is a numbers game. The average advance for an author is $2,500. This means you're giving away a lot of control and ownership of your work for a small advance, nothing that rivals Prince Harry's. But what

---

[29] Nardine Saad, "Prince Harry's 'Spare' Ghostwriter Defends Book's Mistakes as it Breaks Sales Records," *Los Angeles Times*, January 12, 2023, https://www.latimes.com/entertainment-arts/books/story/2023-01-12/prince-harry-spare-errors-ghostwriter-sales.

PRH knew is that if they could buy the rights to Prince Harry's story, then they would make a lot of money. This is how publishing works.

Now, translating this to the average author, the key question that comes up in this publisher selection process is, what assets do you have to offer a traditional publisher? If that's the path you're looking to go down, that is.

In order to get a traditional publishing deal you'll need a literary agent, and to get a literary agent you'll need to put together a book proposal. A book proposal is essentially the business plan for your book. This will show the publisher everything you're bringing to the table, as well as how you intend to market it. It's a myth that traditional publishers market all of the books they publish. They put their marketing dollars behind a very few, select books, which is why they need you and your marketing power and audience to make them money. Are you starting to see the disadvantages here?

If you're someone who has a large audience of people, say 50,000 people on your mailing list or over 1 million subscribers on a social media platform, you have everything you need to publish your book yourself via self-publishing or hybrid publishing because you'll make much more money on it. It's at this point that traditional publishers become interested because they see that you have a big audience who'll help you move a large volume of books, making them money.

If, on the other hand, you're an author who doesn't have a big mailing list or a lot of connections, it's going to be much harder to grab the attention of a traditional publisher. This isn't to say it's impossible, but it will be a lot harder.

Creative and Editorial Control

As we've covered in previous chapters, traditional publishers are looking to have creative and editorial control over your published book. This goes back to the fact that it's all a numbers game.

At the end of the day, a traditional publisher is looking to sell your book to *their* audience, not support you selling your book to *your* audience. This is a very big mismatch from a success standpoint. How you evaluate the success of your book is going to be very different from how a traditional publisher evaluates its success. This mismatch shows up in how your book is edited, designed, and marketed.

Your vision for the cover of your book, for example, may not matter because the publisher is going to go with what they believe will sell the most books, which again may be to an entirely different audience than the one you're intending to impact. We discussed editorial control in the chapter on censorship; but additional areas that come up could be your book's title or subtitle, which you may have a really specific vision for, that you're then forced to change.

If you're unwilling to compromise in any of these areas, then traditional publishing isn't going to be a suitable path for you. If none of this scares you and you're completely open and receptive to the changes made and direction taken by a traditional publisher, and if you have the assets they're looking for, then traditional publishing could be just what you're looking for.

Royalties

Royalties are another area that has a big impact on what type of publishing path you want to pursue. Royalties are actually a little bit complicated to explain, but I do have a webinar called *Pick Your Path to Publishing* that goes through a royalty breakdown in a way that will allow a little more nuance and context than just the written word. You can watch it by going to https://publishyourpurpose.com/path-publishing-webinar/.

Royalties are the moneys you earn as a result of the sale of your book. If you're working with a publisher, the chances are pretty high that you'll be sharing those royalties with them in some percentage breakdown.

When we look at royalties, we can see a couple of things at play, primarily the business model of the publisher you're considering. If you're planning on self-publishing, you'll retain all of the royalties from the sale of your book because you've done the work yourself.

If you're working with a hybrid publisher, business models vary quite a bit. You may find a hybrid publisher who gets 0 percent in royalties, and you'll talk to another that may take 80 percent. You'll want to look closer at their models. Usually, but not always, a hybrid publisher with a higher upfront fee will take a lower royalty percentage and a hybrid publisher who may not charge a lot upfront for their services might take a higher royalty on the back end. There's no set way to do this and every hybrid operates a bit differently, so you'll want to ensure you know what you're getting when you begin discussions with them. You'll learn more about having these discussions in the next chapter.

Traditional publishing, the path in which you pursue a literary agent to represent you and get a book advance, is where the majority of royalties are kept by the publisher. (Sidebar: an advance is essentially a signing bonus that's paid to the author before the book is published and is paid against future earnings of the book's sales.) They're investing in your book more often than you are and therefore are keeping the majority of the profit from your book on the back end. Additionally, you'll be splitting your royalties with your literary agent who helped you get the book deal in the first place. Often, you'll be splitting 10 percent between you and them. Again, different business models.

Here's a simple visual way to look at how royalties play out:

Self-Publishing	Hybrid Publishing	Traditional Publishing
You keep 100%	You keep the majority (varies)	They keep all <10%

Now let's look at the dollars and cents impact that your publishing path can have on your royalties over the longevity of your book. This is where the catch-22 of traditional publishing feels more evident: by the time you catch the attention of a traditional publisher, you no longer need them. You could do it on your own or work with a hybrid and make significantly more money over the long term.

If you sold 10,000 books through a traditional publisher, your profit would be somewhere around $3,700. With a hybrid publisher you could make $63,500, and with self-publishing you could make $74,700. That

$11,200 difference between self-publishing and hybrid publishing could be the revenue generated from the book that allows you to work with a skilled and professional team to position your book with the ability to sell 10,000 copies to begin with.

	SELF	HYBRID	TRADITIONAL
	$19.95	$19.95	$19.95
Wholesale Discount	40%	40%	40%
Subtotal	$11.97	$11.97	$11.97
Print Cost	$4.50	$4.50	$4.50
Net Royalty	$7.47	$7.47	$7.47
Royalty Total	$7.47	$6.35	$0.37
	^ 100%	^ 85%	^ 5%

When we look at this information in totality, we can see that there are multiple paths to publishing. If you decide upon the traditional route, it's important to remember that you, the author, will be beholden to your publisher for creative control and financial gains while still taking on the lion's share of the marketing yourself. If you opt to go the self-publishing route, the costs are seemingly lower, but your time, energy, and any other resources are your sole responsibility. Often, we don't have time to battle the steep learning curve to figure it all out.

> A traditional publisher is looking to sell your book to *their* audience, not support you selling your book to *your* audience.

There are pros and cons with whichever decision you make. I firmly believe that hybrid publishing is the best of both worlds, but that's what PYP is, so of course I'd say that.

Bottom Line: You Can Do This!

At this point in this book, if you've decided to pursue a traditional publishing path, there are many other books you can find that will help you do that. But the remainder of this book is going to give advice on how to make the most of both self-publishing and hybrid publishing as viable options.

In the next chapter, we'll talk about what questions to ask your prospective publisher to ensure you're picking the best path for you!

GROW
FURTHER

Watch the *Publish Your Purpose Pick Your Path to Publishing Webinar* to further refine which publishing path will be right for you.

Access the webinar here:
https://publishyourpurpose.com/path-publishing-webinar/.

PROMOTE YOUR PURPOSE

Use Polls

The Internet has no shortage of opinions. We all know this, so let's leverage it. As you go through the writing and publishing process, using online polls is a great way to increase engagement with your potential readers and audience. You can post a poll about anything, such as, "I'm debating between three different subtitles; vote on which you like best." You can create a poll on social media platforms like Facebook or Instagram, or you can use software such as SurveyMonkey—the key is to use a platform that feels good for you. This way, your readers feel like they are part of your process because they've provided feedback.

What to Ask a Publisher

CHAPTER 15

Now that you're at the place where it's time to dive deeply into evaluating who you want to work with, this chapter is going to share the top best practices for doing so as well as provide questions to ask the publishing company or service provider you're evaluating.

We haven't spent a lot of time discussing service providers, but they fall under self-publishing. If you're interested in self-publishing, you'll need to hire a lot of different vendors, contractors, or companies to make this happen. Some of the questions to consider asking a publisher are areas you should consider asking a contractor, but not all.

There are many solid, reputable, and high-quality publishers and service providers out there, but finding them among the sea of predatory publishers and companies can be tricky. And when you do find them, how do you know they're a good fit for you?

Let's help you find a reputable publisher that gets you and your book.

First, Research Your Prospective Publisher

Before picking up the phone, sending that first email, or otherwise engaging with a prospective publisher, do your research. It's your job to find out what kind of publisher they are and whether they're reputable and high-quality.

Your first stop should be to check out ALLi, the nonprofit organization for self-publishing authors we touched upon at the end of Chapter 12. Its mission is ethics and excellence in self-publishing. ALLi's Watchdog List

PUBLISH YOUR PURPOSE

Some things to understand at the start of your evaluation is that not all publishers are created equal. You want to ensure that you're looking for is what you're getting. Remember, on the surface it can be hard to tell the differences between a hybrid publisher and a vanity publisher, so take these steps to ensure you're not falling victim to a scam company.

Find Out What Kind of Publisher They Are

If the publisher or their publishers who show up on the ALLi watchdog List, turn to Google. Google a publisher name + scam and review the results. If you find pages of complaints from others, use that as a warning sign that proceed with caution. The best publisher for you is one with a questionable reputation.

Check Google

Google the listed phone number on their website and review the results. Do they come up on fraud or scam phone number lists?

RED	Confirmed scammer and predatory company. Do not proceed.

GREEN, YELLOW, or RED.[30]

---

30 https://www.allianceindependentauthors.org/watchdog/

> Look for hidden fees. Not all publishers and contracts are created equal. If a price looks too good to be true, it probably is.

speak with. Now it's time to ask them direct questions to make your publisher pick.

Take Control and Ask Questions

Harkening back to Chapter 11 where we discussed the unsaid power imbalance and hierarchy in publishing, this is your time to shine. It's your time to take control into your hands and ask these publishers the hard questions. You're interviewing them just as much as they're interviewing you.

It's a common misconception that hybrid publishers having a pay-for-service business model means that they will work with any author. That is simply untrue. Vanity publishers will work with anyone regardless, so this can help weed out the good from the bad at the onset. At PYP, we turn down more business than we take on because it's important for us to stick true to our purpose and mission as a company. If we deviate from that, we'll lose our identity and the brand reputation that we've built.

So let's dive into the questions you should be asking. I'll also include PYP's answers so that you have a sense of how these questions may be answered by others.

1. **What Are Your Publishing Values?**

    Before you ask a prospective publisher for their values, think through your own. Visit www.PublishYourPurpose.com/book-extras to download a worksheet you can write in to answer this question. Make sure that your prospective publisher's values align with yours. What does this publishing house stand for?

    PYP's Publishing Values

    We are an LGBTQ+ and women-owned B Corporation™ with a mission to elevate the voices often excluded from traditional publishing. We strive to be as inclusive and diverse as we possibly can be but recognize there is still work to be done. To date, 69 percent of our authors are women, 46 percent are LGBTQ+, and 24 percent are Black and Indigenous People of Color (BIPOC).

2. **Who Is Your Target Audience?**

This question will give you an idea of what audience base this publisher is marketing to and what types of books they publish. You want to ensure that anyone you're working with is transparent about their process and who they work with.

PYP's Target Audience

Our readers crave new, revolutionary ideas in subject areas ranging from social justice to entrepreneurship. There's no idea too big for the readers of our books, and we do not turn down book ideas because they are "out there" or "too sensitive."

3. **How Does Your Editing Process Work?**

After you submit your manuscript, will you have any further input on what gets changed? Will you be able to review the edits and choose which ones to keep? Will the edits be big-picture or line-by-line? These questions will give you a sense of how much control you'll have over how your words are presented—and ensure you're not being censored.

Other follow-up questions to consider:

- How many people will be working on your book?
- How many staff members will be touching your book during the process?
- Are they accessible when you have questions?
- Do you have regularly scheduled calls to help guide you in the process?

There are many publishers that you'll never speak to. You'll submit your manuscript and it's solely email communication with form templates and canned responses. Depending on your needs as an author, evaluate their answers against your desired level of collaboration.

PYP's Editing Process

As discussed in Chapter 10, at PYP we think it's essential that editors and authors have a connection and that the editor can act as a thought partner to improve upon the author's manuscript.

If your manuscript is accepted, it will undergo a thorough internal review process. You'll then have the opportunity to choose your editor! Among our editors, you're bound to find one who has a connection to your book's subject matter or just matches your vibe. It's essential that you're excited about your editor—trust us, you will be.

Depending on the state of your manuscript, we'll provide developmental editing, copyediting, and proofreading. But don't worry—all edits must be approved by you before they are put into effect. Unlike some other publishing houses, we center the author in the editing process.

4. What Types of Books and Authors Do You Work With?

Different publishers are also experts in publishing certain types of books. Certain publishers only publish fiction books, while others concentrate their focus on health and wellness books. Knowing which types of books a publisher focuses on will help you predict whether your book is likely to be taken on by a given publisher and whether that publisher should make it on your list of potential candidates.

PYP's Books and Authors

We publish non-fiction books and memoirs. Our authors are thought leaders, experts in their fields, and visionaries paving the way to social change—from food security to anti-racism. While we love all kinds of literature, we do not currently publish fiction, poetry, or children's books.

5. May I Speak with Recent Authors?

If a publishing house has a long list of happy and successful authors, that's a great sign. Ask to speak to a recently (within the last three to six months) published author. Will they readily connect you with a recent author? Are there current testimonials on their website from happy authors? If they provide the name of an author, follow up with that person. It'll be worth your time to do so.

Yes, Please!

Our authors love to talk to aspiring authors about their experiences with our publishing house. If you'd like to meet with a recent author, just let us know over email and we can connect you. We also have video and written testimonials throughout our marketing.

6. Who Retains the Rights to My Book during and after Publishing?

Before you sign any contract or deal with a publisher, you should know what rights you'll have to your book, both during *and* after the publishing process. If you don't have the rights during the publishing process, you'll have little say in what changes are made to your manuscript.

Conversely, you may have the rights to your book during the publishing process but not legally own it once it's published. In this case, you wouldn't be able to make any changes to the published work. You also wouldn't be able to market the book without getting your publisher's permission, including putting your own book on your website, giving copies to a friend, or making your book available anywhere else.

PYP's Stance on Ownership

With PYP, you're always in complete ownership of all of your rights. The easiest way to look at it is that we're licensing the rights to your work for a period of time. We don't own them, and we're never going to stop you from maximizing your opportunities. If you have a movie studio looking to use your work in some way, we're going to be there to support you and help guide you in making the fairest and most equitable decision. We are your partners for the long term.

7. **What Happens If I Want to Get Out of My Contract?**

   If you have a bad experience and want to move your book to another publisher, how do they handle that process? Do you have any recourse? Are you able to move your work elsewhere? If you can move it, how many days' notice do you need to provide? Will they charge you a fee to obtain your files? It's often common practice for authors to be charged upward of thousands of dollars to obtain their files if they decide to break their contract and move their book elsewhere.

   PYP's Contract

   If you decide that you no longer wish to publish your book with us, you can get out of the contract without fees or fuss. All we ask is for a 30-day notice so that we can remove your book from distribution and from our systems and prepare and package your files so that you can take your work elsewhere! And we don't charge a fee to do so.

8. **Will I Be Required to Purchase Copies of the Book?**

   Predatory publishers often require authors to purchase a minimum number of copies of their own books. When a publisher's business model is based on profits from print runs, you'll see a minimum requirement of 1,000 books purchased by the author at 50 percent retail price (which can end up being $10,000+). And you'd have to figure out how to store, ship, and sell those books.

   PYP's Environmental Commitment

   At PYP, we do not have a minimum book order requirement. In fact, we operate with an eco-conscious print-on-demand model. We also encourage our authors to err on the side of caution with their first round of printing. Less is more when ensuring there are no typos in the book that you won't want in the next round of printing.

Look for hidden fees. Not all publishers and contracts are created equal. If a price looks too good to be true, it probably is. Many publishers make their money by selling your books to you, not necessarily selling your books to the end reader.

Sidenote: How to Improve the Environmental Impact of Book Publishing

Ask your publisher to print your books on post-consumer recycled paper, which significantly reduces the carbon footprint compared to printing on virgin fiber. Make sure that print-on-demand is included in your contract when vetting a potential publisher. This means that books are only printed when they're guaranteed to be sold, reducing the likelihood of excess. Whether you're self-publishing or working with a hybrid publisher, make sure you factor in time and resources to convert your manuscript into e-reader format (ePUB). No paper is used to make an e-reader, but plastics derived from petrochemicals, minerals, and metals are, some of which are toxic to the earth and people. The process also produces 66 pounds of carbon dioxide and an estimated 299 liters of water. Lastly, work with local printers to prevent unnecessary carbon emissions caused by shipping.

9. **What Is My Royalty Arrangement?**

Ask them how much they pay you in royalties and how much you keep. Ask them if they pay their author royalties on time. This is a common grievance within the publishing industry, where a publisher commits to paying every three months, six months, or annually, and is consistently late in those royalty payments.

PYP Royalties

At PYP we pay our authors 85 percent in royalties. PYP pays royalties every three months and has never been delayed in making payments to our authors.

10. May I Review Your Contract?

Most publishers won't share a contract prior to the negotiation process (though you can always ask for a sample contract!). But once you've reached the negotiation process and gotten your hands on a contract, nothing will give you more clarity than the fine print. Here's what to look for:

- What format will your book be published in?
- What happens if you want to get out of your contract?
- Who retains the rights to your book during and after publishing?
- Who is listed as the copyright holder of your book?
- Will you legally own the book once it's published?
- Will you have to ask permission to make changes to the published work?
- Will you have to ask permission to put your book on your website, give copies to a friend, or make your book available elsewhere?
- What format will your book be published in (don't make any assumptions)? Do you want a physical paperback, with the option to expand to an ebook, audio edition, and/or hardcover? Get it in writing.
- Will you be required to purchase copies of the book?

Can I see PYP's Contract?

Absolutely. We don't hide anything in the fine print. (Reach out and request a contract review at www.publishyourpurpose.com/contact.) Here are some things to keep in mind from our contracts:

- *We offer hardcover, paperback, and ebook formatting for our books. Audiobooks are available upon specific request.*
- *The author always has the rights to their book. The author is always listed as the copyright holder and always legally owns the book when it's published.*

- *If you want to make changes to the work that's already published, you can. We just need to ensure that your edits adhere to our quality requirements.*

- *If you want to put your book on your website, give copies to a friend, or make your book available elsewhere, go for it! We have strategic conversations with our authors to ensure they're leveraging their books in all of the places they can.*

BONUS TIP! Spell Check

A telltale sign of a fly-by-night publisher is how it spells certain words, such as "copyright" and "foreword." If you see "copy write" or "forward," then consider yourself warned—these are red flags. A legitimate publisher spell-checks their emails and website copy and should definitely know how to spell common industry terms.

Bottom Line: You Can Do This!

There are many ways to feel empowered and confident in the publisher selection process. If you start with the questions from this chapter, you'll be in a better position to choose. And now that you're feeling strong and confident about the paths available to you, let's dive into the costs associated with these paths.

GROW FURTHER

Protect yourself in the publishing industry by downloading the 9 Questions to Ask a Publisher blueprint so that you know the right questions to ask to avoid predatory practices in your process.

Access the blueprint here:
https://publishyourpurpose.com/questions-ask-publisher/.

PROMOTE YOUR PURPOSE

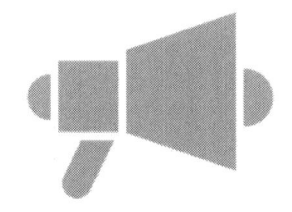

Ask Questions

As an author you aren't expected to know everything about your topic, and your readers certainly don't know everything either. A way to engage your prospective reader is by asking questions. Whether in a newsletter, on social media, or in a lunch-and-learn session you conduct, ask them what they're looking for in your book. This will give them increased buy-in to your book project and increase the likelihood that they'll buy your book when it's available.

CHAPTER 16
Your Publishing Costs

If you dream of one day becoming an author, there are two things you need to do. The first is to make it a priority *now*. (Doing it "later" usually means never.) You're already prioritizing because you're reading this book!

The second is to make sure you don't let money get in the way of your dream. Despite what you may think, publishing your bestseller can be costly, regardless of the publishing path you choose.

Why You Need To Invest In Your Book

Nobody said it would be easy, but it's *definitely* worth it. Publishing a book can be a life accomplishment on its own, a way to increase your reach, and a means to get your big idea out in the world. But in order to go from idea to published book, you'll need to invest time, and yes, money.

To clear up a pretty big myth: there is no publishing route that is completely free. Between the three publishing options—traditional, self-publishing, and hybrid—there are varying costs to see your book go from idea to bookstore shelves.

If you're worried that you can't afford publishing at this time, let's challenge you to see things differently. You, on your own, might not be able to finance your book publishing, but with the right fundraising campaign, you *will* be able to raise the money you need to turn your dream into a reality.

Making an investment in your book is the best thing you can do for your business, nonprofit, or inner child that always dreamed of becoming an author. The effort you put in now to raise the money you need to move forward will absolutely be transformed into a worthy investment.

The Known Costs

Let's dive into the known costs of publishing your book, then we'll circle back to how you can use fundraising to make it happen.

I encourage you to look at writing a book like a business. Look at your book as an investment rather than an expense. My goal is for you to be armed and protected with the right information related to pricing so you're not taken advantage of.

> **Making an investment in your book is the best thing you can do for your business, nonprofit, or inner child that always dreamed of becoming an author.**

MYTHS ABOUT BOOK PUBLISHING COSTS

MYTH	TRUTH
Self-publishing and traditional publishing are the only routes.	There are three main routes: traditional, self, and hybrid publishing.
Traditional publishing houses cover marketing costs.	You'll need to cover marketing and public relations costs out-of-pocket when working with a traditional publisher.
Editing is a one-time effort and a flat rate.	There are four main phases or types of editing and costs vary greatly.
Traditional publishers cover editing costs.	You'll need to cover developmental editing costs, which are often expensive.
You'll make a lot of money from your book once it's published.	A published book isn't a surefire revenue stream, especially if you're self-publishing.
If you work with a traditional publisher, you'll keep all of your royalties.	You need to split your royalties with your literary agent when working with a traditional publisher.
You can easily design your own book cover in Canva or Photoshop.	Unless you're a graphic designer, you need to find professional help for a compelling book cover.
You only need to publish an ebook.	There are many digital and print formats you'll need to consider to ensure sales.
You need a large social media following to publish your book.	You can pay marketing professionals to help build your brand and social media following.
You need to pay a publisher upfront to read your manuscript.	You should never pay a publisher or any other professional upfront to read your book.

Mindset Realignment: Your Book Is an Investment, Not a Cost

The most important shift you can make as a first-time author is to think of your book as an investment, not a cost. The time, energy, and money you invest in your book will yield financial and professional returns (and immeasurable personal returns too).

How You Can Grow Your Money by Publishing a Book

1. You'll sell books.
2. New clients and people will find and hire you.
3. You'll get press and media opportunities that drive sales.
4. You'll get paid higher speaking and consulting rates.

Benefits of Publishing Your Book

- Consulting opportunities
- Speaking engagements
- Higher rates for speaking and consulting
- Brand awareness
- Expertise establishment
- Published author status!
- Childhood dream fulfillment
- Connection with people at your level
- Greater impact of your mission and purpose
- Sharing of your story and work with the world

How to Plan Your Book Publishing Investment

Step 1: Decide Your Publishing Path

Explore the upfront costs, royalties, and bottom lines of the three publishing models: traditional, self-publishing, and hybrid publishing.

Traditional Publishing

Traditional publishing, as we've been discussing, is working with name-brand publishers, usually the NYC kind. There are no upfront costs related to publishing. However, you'll need to invest your own money to cover

- editing costs, particularly developmental editing;
- marketing; and
- public relations efforts.

Royalties are low, ranging from 4–10 percent. You'll split your royalties with your literary agent who secured your publishing agreement. Typically, you'll make about $0.40 per book (i.e., you'll split roughly $1 per book with your literary agent).

Traditional publishers are seeking authors who have an established brand and platform that will guarantee a large volume of sales. You'll have less creative control, and you'll need to find a literary agent to represent you.

Self-Publishing

Self-publishing success depends on who you hire and what you're willing to spend. The upfront costs can range from $150 to $70,000 (yes, I've spoken to people who've spent up to $70,000 on their book doing it themselves—mainly because they had to go back and undo a lot of work once they realized what they didn't know about the process). You'll need to budget for the following areas: cover design, editing, formatting, project management, marketing strategy, and marketing services. You'll probably also need a new or updated website, promotional materials, and social media support.

You'll receive 100 percent of the royalties for each book you sell, depending on the printing costs and where you sell (e.g., directly versus on a third-party platform like Amazon). However, you'll need to project manage yourself. *You* are responsible for publishing a book to industry standards and building your brand name. And *you* are responsible for knowing where to find information on those standards.

Hybrid Publishing

Hybrid publishing is a happy medium: it integrates the support of a traditional publisher with creative freedom and higher returns of self-publishing. With hybrid publishing, the upfront costs range from $2,000 to $150,000, and the royalties range from 15–85 percent. These are wide ranges, so selecting the right hybrid publisher makes all the difference.

Hybrid publishers complement your strengths, have a catalog of experienced and trusted professional experts to help you, and guide you through the publishing process so you're not alone, fending for yourself in the wild, Wild West of publishing!

The Bottom Line by Publishing Type

The numbers and information on the following page are estimates based on PYP industry knowledge for a 150-page book (approximately 35,000 words).

YOUR PUBLISHING COSTS

Publishing Type	Upfront Costs	Royalties	Bottom Line	Wild Cards
Traditional	Zero	4-10% split with your literary agent	$0.40 per book	• Marketing + PR costs • Less creative control • Literary agent representation
Self-Publishing	$150-$70,000	100%	$10 per book	• All the creative control • Holding yourself accountable + meeting deadlines • If you don't meet industry standards, you risk damage to your brand and reputation
Hybrid Publishing	$2,000-$150,000	15-85% with most authors receiving around 50%	$1.50-$8.50 per book	• Finding the right hybrid publisher fit to complement your skills • Creative freedom • Project management to help you reach "published author" status
Publish Your Purpose*	$18,000-$22,000 *Price varies based on publishing needed	85%	Usually around $8.50 per book	We've got the wild cards covered!

235

Step 2: What You Need to Produce a High-Quality Book

There are major discrepancies between publishing models and among publishing houses and experts. You might see a book cover design being sold for $5 or $5,000. We know these ranges are overwhelming, and we want to share the best practices we've learned along the way.

Self-Publishing Services to Invest In

1. Cover design
2. Editing
3. Formatting
4. Project management
5. Marketing strategy
6. Marketing services

You cannot cut corners on cover design and editing. The cover design gets your reader interested—and editing keeps them reading. Going the DIY route for these services may tragically impact your book publishing credibility, sales, brand, and future.

1. Cover Design

Range: $5–$5,000
Recommendation: $1,500

Book covers are the critical entry points for readers: they catch their eyes, inspire their imagination, and give them a sense of who you are. And you get what you pay for when it comes to cover design. (If you currently have Fiverr or Canva up in a browser tab, stop. Don't do it.) We've found that $1,200–$1,500 is the sweet spot for cover designs that make you proud and stand the test of time.

2. Editing

Range: $100–$10,000
Recommendation: $6,000

The editing beast! There are four types of editing:

1. Developmental
2. Line
3. Copy
4. Proofread

They are all equally important and require different skill sets. If you're self-publishing, please remember how hard it is to objectively edit your own work. It's hard for your brain to edit something you've written and read a thousand times. In our experience, you'll need upward of $6,000 to edit a book thoroughly. Remember, words on a page live forever, and how your book flows will keep readers turning the pages.

3. Print and Digital Formatting

Range: $100–$3,000
Recommendation: $2,200

Formatting is critical to book distribution and access. Formatting the book for different file types or print sizes requires design support. Print designers are called typesetters or interior designers. The cost for print formatting ranges from $100–$3,000. Ebook designers may charge $1–$3 per page to convert your book to a digital format. We've found $2,200 is an effective price point for creating optimal print and digital formatting options and that $1,600 for print and $600 for ebooks are the sweet spots—a combined $2,200—for making sure your book is accessible and enjoyable.

4. Project Management

Range: $0-$14,000
Recommendation: $5,000

We've seen the magic of project managers time and again. The publishing process has many moving parts, from purchasing an ISBN number to securing marketing assistance. A project manager keeps track of all the moving parts—including you! Their purpose is to ensure you reach your goal of publishing. They typically charge by the hour, and their rates are anywhere from $35–$75 per hour—and they need roughly 100–200 hours to work their magic from start to finish.

5. Marketing Strategy

Range: $0-$40,000
Recommendation: $10,000

A comprehensive marketing strategy will solidify your brand and presence as an author and prepare a detailed book launch—both critical to your success as an author. At the very least, we recommend a solid book launch. A marketing strategy is the most important part of the marketing process.

6. Marketing Services

Range: $0-$20,000
Recommendation: $5,000

Marketing services are the catch-all of book publishing. Here are some things that fall under "marketing services":

- Personal brand logo
- Choosing and securing your website domain
- Creating an online course to complement your book
- Pitching you and your book to be featured on podcasts

An effective marketing strategy will help you find paths toward more exposure and revenue.

Step 3: Calculate Your Total Investment for Your Book

Check out the book ROI calculator on our website to help you do the math for you! You can access it at https://publishyourpurpose.com/book-publishing-revenue-calculator/.

PUBLISHING SERVICE	LOW END	HIGH END	IDEAL SPEND	YOUR BUDGET
Cover Design	$5	$5,000	$1,500	
Editing	$100	$10,000	$6,000	
Formatting	$50	$3,000	$2,200	
Project Management	$0	$14,000	$5,000	
Marketing Strategy	$0	$40,000	$10,000	
Marketing Services	$0	$20,000	$5,000	
TOTAL	$155	$92,000	$29,700	

Our range at Publish Your Purpose is between $18,000-$22,000, which varies based on publishing needs.

Your Publishing Path Is Up To You

Ultimately, your published words are a reflection of you. You need to be comfortable with your investment and your published book. Marketing is often the area that authors try to skimp on, but the reality is that no one is going to magically find your book unless you're putting the work in to help your reader find it. Marketing isn't something to be skipped, as visibility for your book is imperative to finding readers to experience the transformation you wish them to seek.

If you're feeling a little overwhelmed or shocked by how much of an investment your book will be, let's talk about how to tackle that from both a monetary and marketing standpoint.

What Your Book Funding Can Do

The funding that you raise for your book can go to a multitude of things, from the beginning of the writing process to the cost of professional editors. Here are some ideas!

- **Writing Support**
  If you've recently decided that you want to write a book, but have yet to finish a manuscript, you can join a six-month-long course to help you finish your manuscript.

- **Publishing Support**
  If you have a manuscript that's ready for publishing, you can apply to become an author with PYP, a hybrid publisher of non-fiction books that seeks to make a difference.

- **Professional Help**
  If you need help after your manuscript is written, you can seek out professionals in cover design, editing, formatting, project management, marketing strategy, marketing services, website design or updating, promotional materials creation, and social media support.

Five Tips on Crowdfunding for Authors

1. Change Your Mindset

You don't need to throw your life savings into your book, and you don't need to publish your book alone. There are people (your community, following, family) who want to see your big idea come to fruition. Your connections want you to succeed, and you'll be surprised by how much they'll donate and offer you to help see your dreams fulfilled.

Fundraising expert Mary Valloni puts it this way: "Money has so much emotion tied to it and I am extremely passionate about ending the scarcity mindset."[31] Instead of worrying about asking too much of your connections, believe that an investment in your book will have a positive impact on the world. If you believe it, they will too!

2. Share Your Why

Answer the question: *Why would anybody want to fund this book? Why would anybody want to be a part of the work that I'm doing?* Once you have your "why" you can begin to reach out to your network and get other people inspired.

When talking with people, tell them what your book is going to be able to do and the kind of impact you envision for it. Conversations have a multiplying effect on motivation and inspiration. The more you talk about your book, the more excited you'll become, and the more excited your community (the people who will fund your book) will become. And once they're excited, they'll reach out to their connections. They'll want to be a part of your vision too.

Don't stop at your friends and family or immediate community. If you have a thriving social following or clientele, tell them that you're writing a book! This will not only hold you accountable for actually following through with your goal, but will add to your book's hype.

You need to build the suspense, *the hype*, and the attention. Once your book is released, you'll want to have already built a sizable following and a group of people who've been waiting for its release.

3. Start the Cover Process Early

In order to build said "hype," you'll need a beautiful book cover. In fact, marketing for your book can't start until you have one. If you're thinking, *What? A book cover? I haven't even written the book yet!* let me explain. As we already explored, in order to fund your book, you'll need to get a lot of people on board. People need to believe that this book will actually come to fruition, and in order to see it be successful, they need

---
31 https://maryvalloni.com/

to see what it's going to look like. The old saying, "Don't judge a book by its cover," is dandy and all, but we all know that we do judge books (at least in part) by the quality of their covers.

One of the first things we do with our authors at PYP is begin to develop the *perfect* book cover. We work with professional book designers to get the right look for your big idea.

4. Use a Crowdfunding for Authors Platform

There are countless crowdfunding platforms that exist for the exact purpose of helping you raise the money you need to publish your book. Here are a few of our favorites:

- Publishizer
- Indiegogo
- GoFundMe
- Kickstarter
- Patreon

Essentially, what you're doing with this crowdfunding platform is finding people who are willing (and excited) to pay for your book ahead of time. We call this a "pre-order campaign" and you can get really creative with how to go about it.

5. Launch a Pre-Order Campaign

A pre-order (or pre-sale) is simply selling your book in advance of your publication date. While there are two ways to pre-order, we recommend setting up a pre-order campaign through your website in order to fund the publishing of your book.

Though you can set up a pre-order campaign on Amazon, you won't have access to the funds until the book is live, so it only helps if you already have enough funding to get the book published! Plus, your pre-order campaign can help you obtain the donor's contact information to build an email list and, eventually, convert your readers into your sales funnel.

There are tons of different creative ways to sell pre-orders. Here are some of our favorites:

- Ask dedicated readers to donate $50 now, and once the book comes out they'll not only be one of the first people to get their hands on a copy but will get a signed copy.

- For big donations (over $1,500), you can offer the opportunity to have their name appear in the acknowledgments. Having their name acknowledged in a printed book and feeling like a part of the process can be a really exciting prospect for anyone.

- Let's say there's an organization that aligns with your book directly or indirectly (think: a book on climate change, and a nonprofit organization that aims to restore the polar bear population in Alaska). You could offer them 1,000 books at $8 apiece. That's $8,000 for your publishing needs.

- Other ideas include adding a signed poster or a few tickets to a book launch event to the donation to get your readers excited to join in.

Pre-ordering your book can have a huge impact on your ability to make your dream of being an author a reality, as well as set the strong groundwork for getting people interested and excited so that your marketing is easier as you go forward.

Bottom Line: You Can Do This!

Publishing a book is an investment that, if done right, can provide a return for years to come. You don't have to let money get in the way of your dream of becoming a published author. If you can implement a few powerful marketing strategies at the start of the process, then the *how* you'll make the investment will sort itself out.

GROW
FURTHER

Understand your full publishing cost by downloading the Book Cost Blueprint so that you know exactly how to allocate your resources.

Access the blueprint here:
https://publishyourpurpose.com/book-cost-blueprint-optin/.

PROMOTE YOUR PURPOSE

Start a Street Team

Gathering your best clients, fans, or friends and intentionally giving them a role in relation to your book can be a powerful asset to leverage later. Creating a "Street Team," a "hype group," or whatever you may want to call it, is a great way to gather your fans into one group and brainstorm how to help you promote your book once it's available.

It may be hard to think about someone being "a fan" of your work, but I assure you there are people out there who are fans of yours and would be honored to be part of an intimate club of people helping support you and your book launch.

CHAPTER 17
Your Publishing Timeline

How long it takes to publish your book is very much dependent on which publishing path you choose. It can be as little as 30 days (which I strongly advise against for putting any thought leadership into the world), or as long as three to five years. Let's explore these publishing timelines in a little more detail.

How Long Does it Take to Publish a Book?

Whether you're publishing with a hybrid publisher or self-publishing, getting your book into your reader's hands takes time. How long this process takes depends on a number of things—from how long it takes you to write your manuscript to the editing of your book. Here are some of the major components of the book publishing process and their respective timelines.

Writing and Editing

The first thing you need to do is finish writing your manuscript. The writing process takes as long as you need it to, so sticking to a schedule for writing will keep you on track and make sure that you meet your deadlines and complete your manuscript. Refer back to Part 2 of this book for ideas on how to create a deadline and stick with it.

Month One

The first month is typically spent on the developmental editing stage. This means having an editor look over your manuscript from a 30,000-foot view. At this stage, they'll help you with identifying any gaps in the framework of your manuscript and look to ensure the chapters you currently have are in the right order, if new chapters need to be added, or even if a whole chapter should be deleted.

I personally had this happen while writing *Beyond the Rainbow*. My editor (who was also a friend) sent me a text that said, "RIP Chapter 7." At first I was upset about the idea that I had to delete an entire chapter, but upon reviewing it and seeing what she meant, I knew she was right and thus deleted the chapter. May Chapter 7 rest in peace.

At PYP, we also focus on the cover design of your book within the first month or two. We see the power and value of having a cover design early from a marketing standpoint. Not all publishers will have an emphasis on marketing first, so refer back to what you've decided your publishing needs, wants, and desires to be. What we need to begin the cover design process is knowing with certainty what your book's title and subtitle will be. Once that's done, the design process can begin.

When it comes to titles and subtitles, we often work with authors who are absolutely certain what their title will be but are lost on the subtitle. There's a lot of strategy that goes into a strong title and subtitle pairing, and that has a direct impact on the success of your book. At PYP we pay a lot of attention to this area. We also have a group of 1,000 readers and aspiring authors that we run ideas by to crowdsource feedback and gain additional insights on several aspects of the publishing process.

Month Two

The second month is when you begin planning your larger marketing campaign. While this is happening, you're still editing your book. This is the line editing phase. A line editor is reviewing your book paragraph by paragraph and line by line. They're ensuring that all of your thoughts within each chapter are in the right order, that you're making your points, and that you're ultimately delivering on the promise of your book to your readers. This is also when you would start collecting testimonials and, potentially, a foreword for your book.

> Whether you're publishing with a hybrid publisher or self-publishing, getting your book into your reader's hands takes time.

Month Three

The third month is when you begin working with a copy editor. A copy editor reviews your book for the nitty-gritty details of grammar and punctuation. This is also when you look at ways in which you can market your book before it's available to your readers. These tasks include setting up a website, logo, social media account, headshots, and email marketing. These are things that will help you effectively market your book and get your audience hyped about it before your book launch.

The final phase of editing, often occurring within months three or four, is proofreading. This is the final set of eyes on your book to ensure all the Is are dotted and the Ts are crossed before it moves into the interior layout phase.

Publishing Logistics & Marketing Strategy

Months Four & Five

Once the proofreading phase is finished and your marketing foundation has been set, months four and five will be when you design your book's interior and do additional work on your marketing strategy.

The design of your book includes the interior layout, also known as typesetting, and any illustrations, charts, graphs, or pictures that are included. If you don't have a designer already in mind and aren't a graphic designer, do not try to do your own design.

As your book continues to be developed and gets closer to the finished product, you want to continue updating your website and social media about the progress. Taking your audience along for the ride will generate hype about your book and keep them engaged. This also updates them on a timeline of when your book is expected to be released. One common marketing idea is to offer them a chapter of your book for free if they sign up for your email list or follow you on social media.

During this time you also want to consider where your audience is and how you're going to reach them (refer back to the work you did in the earlier part of this book). In other words, what social media platforms are they on, what do they listen to, and where do they shop? Blindly marketing on every platform you can name *may* get you results, but focusing your marketing and advertising efforts will make more people aware and hyped up about your book. For example, if you're writing a book about health and wellness and your readers are also listeners of podcasts, then finding wellness podcasts and getting on them as a guest will be more effective than promoting your book via tweets on Twitter.

Marketing Execution

Month Six & Beyond

Month six should be about focusing on all of the marketing plans you've been making. Make sure that you're sticking to a schedule for emails and social media posts and appearing on all relevant (social) media platforms. You want to make connections and schedule time as a guest to appear on podcasts, radio shows, and guest blogs. The more you can leverage the connections you have to engage your audience directly, the better.

Month seven is when you continue to get people hyped up about your book launch. Ideally, your book should be complete or just about complete. You're sticking to the schedule that you made for yourself and continuing to leverage the connections that you've built up during the publishing process to promote your book.

Month eight is your book launch! Take a moment to relish the work that you've put in and the fact that people will read your book. This doesn't mean that everything just stops at this point. You want to continue to promote and advertise your book for the next few months, riding the momentum from your book launch and making new connections with businesses, people, and readers. The day of your book launch isn't the finish line, it's actually the starting line. This is where the fun begins—creating impact and changing the world with your book!

> Blindly marketing on every platform you can name *may* get you results, but focusing your marketing and advertising efforts will make more people aware and hyped up about your book.

Bottom Line: You Can Do This!

As I mentioned earlier, this is an average timeline that we use at PYP. Each publisher or service provider will have their own version of this timeline, and it may or may not align with what you've read here. If timing is important and you're trying to get your book out to your readers quickly, take that into consideration when you're choosing the right publisher for you.

All timelines are estimates, and how quickly you move through one phase will depend on how quickly you can start that next phase. As a result, a standard six-to-eight-month timeline could end up being a four-to-six-month timeline for one author or an eight-to-ten-month timeline for another, depending on who your support team is and how much they'll prioritize a quick release with you.

GROW FURTHER

Download the Publish Your Purpose workbook so that you can map out your book publishing timeline.

Access the workbook here:
https://publishyourpurpose.com/book-extras.

PROMOTE YOUR PURPOSE

Prepare an Elevator Pitch

The more you tell people that you're writing a book, the more questions you'll be asked. Now is a great time to prepare your elevator pitch so you can succinctly describe what your book is about in the time it takes for you to get from the floor you're on down to the lobby. Brevity will become your friend as you go from explaining your book concept to people you know to describing it on a podcast when you're a guest.

Your Book Launch + Beyond

It's often assumed that once you're at the phase of launching your book, you're done; the task is over, the book is published, and readers will find it. However, that is simply not true. Book writing and publishing is a three-phase race: you cross the finish line of writing, then cross the finish line of publishing, but there's no finish line of marketing—it's a consistent and ongoing process.

The books that sell the most and make the biggest impact are the ones that the author is constantly out talking about and doing something with. This isn't to say that this has to be fancy or sophisticated marketing, but you have to be out there talking about your book.

A Strategic Lens

From a strategic lens, if you created your book with intention and positioned it as the center of your professional universe, the ability to market it in an ongoing way is going to be a lot easier. Your book should be the tip of your marketing spear, the center of your marketing universe, the sun around which your book business/company marketing orbits.

When we're incredibly thoughtful and intentional about how everything interconnects, our marketing doors open wide up. Revisit the early chapters of this book to remind yourself what your goals are for your book, what your mission is, and what your purpose is—the answers to those questions will help you get to the bottom of the bigger messaging and positioning of your book so that it can be the center of your marketing ecosystem.

What You Don't Want to Look Like

The benefits of writing a book are so expansive that, even within this book, we've really just scratched the surface. But I want to use a networking example to explain how a book can reposition and change everything for you.

Tell me if you've ever experienced this at a networking event: You're talking to someone who was a realtor when you previously met them, but this time you connect with them and they tell you about a new product they're selling (let's say it's essential oils). You walk away from this interaction because you didn't realize they jumped from being a realtor to selling products instead, and you chalk it up to people evolving and changing in their businesses and interests. Then you run into this person about a week later at a different networking event. This time you overhear them talking about getting into feng shui and how they recently helped someone remodel their rental property to be more intentional and mindful of how their environment is set up and how it impacts their guest experience. Now you're even more confused because you first thought they were a realtor, then switched your perception to the fact that they now sell essential oils, but now you're overhearing them talking about remodeling office spaces for feng shui. You may be thinking, *What the heck does this person actually do?*

Let me ask you…would you ever want to be on the receiving end of that question? Someone enthusiastically engaging you and asking you what you do is very different from someone genuinely being confused as to what it is you do in this world. This isn't going to help you get business or see the results you're hoping for.

But if you're a strategic storyteller, you can control this narrative completely and ensure that no one is confused by what you do. If this fictitious person were to have interwoven the components of their story and what they do, there'd be no confusion. Come to find out this person still is a realtor but sells essential oils and is helping people feng shui their physical spaces, and their superpower is that they use essential oils to help calm the nerves of homeowners as they're going through the buying process. Their knowledge of room design for maximum impact helps them create a vision for what their clients' potential homes might look like.

> Book writing and publishing is a three-phase race: you cross the finish line of writing, then cross the finish line of publishing, but there's no finish line of marketing—it's a consistent and ongoing process.

Which person would you rather show up with? The power of a book is that this person could have written a book that speaks to all three areas and their intersectionality rather than coming across as disjointed or disconnected in networking environments. The book is truly the tip of the spear to help laser focus someone toward what it is that you do, especially if it directly ties into how you show up in the world each and every day.

What Does Your Book Launch Look Like?

It can be inspiring and exciting to think about what your book launch will look like once your book is ready for your readers to consume. Now is the time to think about both short-term book launch excitement and long-term book marketing plans. If you don't have a proper marketing strategy in place or a book launch plan, your book can get lost in the shuffle of everything that you have to do professionally, and you won't be able to reach your reader.

At PYP, we've had authors launch books in what feels like every type of configuration. From the author who rents a room at a local restaurant and invites friends and family to come and celebrate to the author who spends $25,000 to rent out a prominent theater—I believe we've seen it all. The number one most important thing here is to do what feels right for you and aligns with you. Now is not the time to be "keeping up with the Joneses." And book launching isn't just one-and-done; it's a series of activities that align with your book and reader.

Book Launch Example 1: *Beyond the Rainbow*

Back in 2017 when I was launching *Beyond the Rainbow*, my book launch was made super easy! I was invited to be a guest speaker on a panel, alongside a few colleagues, in NYC in June (LGBTQ+ pride month). All I had to do was wheel a suitcase full of books into a gorgeous office building of Penn Mutual in Manhattan and launch my book to an audience of 70+ people. I didn't have to arrange the location, find a caterer, or really market to my audience that wasn't in the general Connecticut or NYC area.

Book Launch Example 2: *House on Fire*

In 2020 when I was launching my memoir *House on Fire*, I was severely limited in my options as a result of COVID-19. Rather than host any type of in-person event, I opted for doing a virtual book club tour. It was glorious. I had a chance to meet a number of really cool people who were doing really cool things as part of their established book clubs. My role here was to organize my calendar to get it to work with the schedule of the book clubs. It was not a lot of work but required administration skills to make it happen. But again, different books, different style launches.

Book Launch Example 3: *Publish Your Purpose*

This book that you're reading had a very different launch plan. This book launched as part of our annual "Business of Becoming an Author" community event. We invited our authors from all over the country to come speak about their book on panels and the local Hartford, CT, community to support them. On September 27, 2023, this book launched at the famous Mark Twain House as part of this celebratory event. The focus of the event is on our authors, not us as a company, and this book was part of the backdrop of the overall event.

Pre-Book-Launch Steps

Let's talk through a very high-level idea of what your book launch plan *could* look like. Remember, every book launch is a little different and you'll want to do what works best for you and your readers. Just because someone is doing something to launch their book does not mean you need to do the same thing. Do your homework and research, and make sure your launch aligns with your goals as an author.

These steps aren't going to be as specific, but rather an idea of what you could be doing from a marketing standpoint in the months leading up to your book being available to readers. What I'll say here is that it's *never* too soon to start marketing your forthcoming book—*ever*. The longer lead time you have, the better.

Before Publishing

Before publishing, make a concerted effort to let people know that you've written your book. You can start marketing your book well before it's written. It's common that a book is marketed before it's completed, as we discussed in Chapter 16. The two most important items you need to begin marketing at this phase are your book cover and your book description. Once you have these items, you're smooth sailing!

Your Book Cover

When it comes to your book cover, there's a lot of strategy in picking the one that will best serve your readers and your marketing. But for the sake of this conversation, let's assume you have strategically thought through how your cover is going to engage your readers (thinking about such things as weaving in your business or professional branding to create a sense of cohesion). What you'll want to do next is post your cover everywhere. Start telling everyone in your network that your book is coming.

Once people see a book cover, they immediately feel that your book is real and tangible, even if your book isn't yet fully written or ready to be published. You'll want to have a vague idea of when your book will be published and share that alongside your newly designed cover. Ideally, you'll want to go with a season and year. For example, "I'm super excited to share that my book will be available in fall 2025." Give yourself more time than you need. Readers will never be upset that your book came out earlier than they believed it would, but they *will* be upset if you don't meet your launch date.

Once you get further along in the publishing process, you'll be able to narrow your launch date down. It may go from fall 2025 to October 2025 to the second week of October 2025, to October 11, 2025. In the months leading up to your launch, you'll be able to refine your date. And each time you do, you get your readers further excited about the fact that your book is coming out. Each change in your timeline is an opportunity to share with your readers and get them enthused!

Your Book Description

As you start to promote the fact that your book is coming, you'll want to have your book description ready. This is one of those areas where you really should hire an expert to write this for you. We're often way too close to our own work, so writing our own book description can absolutely be detrimental. You want the outside eye of a copywriting professional who can truly capture what your book is about from a number of different angles. They'll help you capture the essence of your book in a succinct way that really helps the reader understand the promise and premise of your book.

A skilled copywriter will be able to support you in your book description, but ideally you'll want to contract with someone who writes book descriptions specifically. It can be hard to distill down into 300 words or less what your 50,000-word book is about. But a skilled book description copywriter will have no trouble doing this for you.

Your book's description is the first thing your potential readers see (beyond the cover). If you don't capture them or pull them in immediately, you'll lose that potential sale of your book and the ability to positively impact that person's life. We didn't discuss this expense in Chapter 16, but expect to pay somewhere close to $500 for someone to write your book description for you. Do not shortcut this part of the process—it'll be worth every penny of your investment.

Pre-Sales

Now that you have both a professionally designed book cover and book description, the sky's the limit in terms of marketing. Those are the two most important items for marketing because they are the two things your readers need in order to make a decision on whether they're going to purchase your book.

What this also does for you is open up your options for pre-selling your book. Pre-sales or pre-orders are exactly as they sound—the ability for your reader to purchase your book in advance of it being published. What is great about pre-orders is that they allow you to point people to a specific call to action in your pre-launch marketing efforts. They tell your readers exactly what you want them to do, which is to buy your book in advance. This can make your readers feel awesome and special because they're getting inside access to buy the book before the general public.

There are a lot of nuances around pre-sales, but the most important takeaways for you are that 1) they give you strong engagement opportunities with your potential readers, and 2) they help you raise the money you need to invest in the publishing process of your book. So rather than reap the rewards of the sales coming in after your book is published, pre-sales will help you fund your book. It's a win–win.

Pick Your Platforms Wisely

A big part of book marketing is picking your platforms wisely. Social media often remains a big part of an author's marketing strategy, but not for every book. Many experts say "Be everywhere!" when it comes to where to focus your marketing dollars. But the reality is that you need to focus on the platforms where you'll find your ideal clients. Reference Chapter 5 on target readers to give you insight on which platforms you should focus your energies on.

If you don't feel your readers are on Facebook, then don't waste your time on that platform. If you feel your readers are on TikTok, then be on that platform. Just be as intentional as you can about which platforms you invest your time in. Over the years, PYP has been on a lot of platforms, but we decided to condense our efforts down to really focus on our LinkedIn presence and our Publish Your Purpose Author Lab Facebook group. Beyond those two, we have a very limited presence elsewhere. This was an intentional choice based on our data.

Once you decide where you're going to focus your marketing, you can begin sharing information about your forthcoming book. You may have decided that building your email list is your primary book promotion strategy, and that's fantastic (building your email list is always a top recommendation because you're building your audience in something that you can control rather than being at the mercy of a social media algorithm change). You'll want to do everything you can to align your promotion efforts with the platform you've chosen. This will help you ensure strategy and synergy across your marketing.

After Publishing

Intentionally targeting awareness days and/or months can come both before publishing and after publishing, depending on the time frame you're launching within. You'll want to pay attention to what's being talked about on social media and in the news. For example, October is Breast Cancer Awareness Month. If you have a book that can tie into that specific cause, it'll give you an opportunity to enhance your marketing efforts around that specific time. May is Mental Health Awareness Month, and the same thing holds true; if this ties into any theme in your book, you can use it as an opportunity to share something about your book that's related to this topic.

There are also a series of awareness days or weeks—honestly, there's an awareness day for literally everything at this point, or so it seems. And what's really awesome is that if that day doesn't exist, *you* can create it! Whether it's National Donut Day, World AIDS Day, or Teacher Appreciation Week, if you can tie the subject matter of your book into one of these days, it gives you a chance to speak about the connection between that awareness and what you've written about.

Award-Winning or Bestselling?

Throughout the launching process, there should be intentionality in what your goal might be. If we refer back to Chapter 2, what are your personal, professional, and/or business goals? Having your book be a bestseller is often one of the top goals and measures of success for first-time authors.

Bestseller status can take you far. The average reader (and honestly, first-time author) has no idea how the process works or how easily attainable it is with the right strategy. It isn't complicated, but it is time-consuming. If it's something you want to go for, then just do it! You can pay someone to help you do it, or you can do it yourself with the right time commitment to getting it done. But I challenge you to think about another option.

How would it feel to be able to call yourself an "award-winning author"? When it comes to bestselling authors, many people can say that—including myself. About 70 percent of books that PYP publishes are also bestsellers. But what we've noticed is that being an award-winning author can get you a bit more credibility because it's less common and harder to achieve. With bestsellers, the system can essentially be gamed because there's an exact formula to follow to get those results. But when it comes to award-winning status, it isn't that easy.

Reputable book awards across the globe have a strong vetting process to identify what books are a fit for an award versus which aren't. I'm fortunate enough to be a book judge for a large award contest and, for this particular one, there are three judges for every book that spans both content and design. One of the benefits of submitting for awards is that often the judges will provide feedback to the authors and publishers of the books submitted. This is fantastic because it also gives you feedback on what you're doing awesomely or where you may have missed the mark and subsequently aren't receiving an award.

There are lists of available book award options scattered across the internet, so you'll want to do some research to see whether there's one that your book is suitable for. Most awards have submission fees because managing and judging an awards contest can be incredibly time-consuming for everyone involved, including the organizers and volunteers reviewing the books.

Produce an Audiobook

A great way to leverage your book launch is to stagger the release of your audiobook. There are two ways books are most commonly released: 1) all book formats come out at once, including paperback, hardcover, ebook, and audiobook; and 2) stagger the release of your versions. Sometimes you'll see an ebook come out, followed by a paperback or hardcover a couple of months later, followed by an audiobook six to nine months after that. There are pros and cons to each of these release schedules, and it's entirely up to you to determine which makes the most sense for you. Ideally, you'll be working with a team of people who can help support that process and identify what the best path for you will be.

But what's fantastic about a staggered audiobook is that it gives you a reason to go out to your network again with a message that's something to the effect of, "Hey, my book is now available in audiobook. Go get it now!"

Readers have different reading preferences, so if you had people waiting for you to release an audiobook, you'll be able to scoop up a bunch of sales in this launch phase.

Create a Workbook

A workbook is a fantastic opportunity to further engage your readers. You can do a workbook style similar to how I've scattered the link to our workbook throughout this entire book. This is so that any reader can access it by visiting www.PublishYourPurpose.com/book-extras. An alternative method is to charge someone for your workbook. In your book you reference the workbook that can be obtained from your website or online retailer, and in the workbook you reference back to the book. This provides you with two books to move your readers between, essentially making you a little extra money per reader and also helping your readers have a better chance at the transformation you're hoping they achieve.

Create an Online Program

A natural extension of a book is to create an online program. Online programs often dovetail directly with the contents of a book. The biggest benefit of a book when it comes to online programs is that, since you've spent countless hours of time and energy creating a book flow and format that helps your readers learn something, you already have the outline and structure of your online program or course and can simply adapt your book's chapters to serve that function.

This is not to say that there isn't a lot of hard work involved in creating an online program or course, but you have one of the hardest parts done—the framework. Earlier and throughout this book, I've mentioned our Getting Started for Authors writing program, which is directly tied to Part 2. If you're really eager to get your book strategically written within six months and with the support of a team, then this type of program could be for you. If you make this offer to your readers because you've created something that continues to help them directly solve their problems, you'll see a conversion of people coming over from the book to your program.

The entire purpose here is to help your readers solve their problem. Often a book alone will solve your readers' problem, but sometimes readers are looking for additional support from you. An interactive online program or course could be just the thing to take their learning experience to the next level.

Speaking, Consulting, and Other Revenue-Generating Activities

At the beginning of this book we talked about your vision and goals. Your goals may have included gaining new consulting business, promoting a new speaking business, or perhaps launching some kind of product. Whatever the revenue-generating activity may be, this is a continuation of your book's marketing activities.

When you promote your book, you're also promoting everything else that you do, which includes all of these items and then some! Don't limit yourself with how you can use your book to help you generate streams of income within your business; the sky is truly the limit.

What's My End Game?

My end goal for you throughout this entire book has been engagement. Engagement looks different for every reader. At PYP we have many free resources for you to participate in, and what's attractive to one person won't be attractive to another. This is how it should be. Think through what's going to be most beneficial to your readers. See where there are opportunities to provide them with more information, take their learning a step further, engage with you meaningfully and personally, schedule time with you to see if they could work with you, and on and on and on…There are so many options.

Bottom Line: You Can Do This!

After you've finished writing your book, make sure you go through it, reread it, be mindful, and be intentional as to where you may be able to create an opportunity for your readers to engage with you. It's my hope that I showed this by example throughout the entirety of this book. This book has intentionally been a blueprint, a framework, a formula for you to emulate. After all, I have to talk the talk and walk the walk—and what fun would it be if I didn't do that here?

GROW FURTHER

Go back through this book and review the "Promote Your Purpose" section at the end of each chapter. Then put the appropriate next steps and tips into action.

PROMOTE YOUR PURPOSE

Revisit What You've Learned

In this chapter we discussed the variety of options available to you when it comes to marketing your book. Take time to revisit the steps and tips to determine the next move that makes the most sense for your book and your goals.

Conclusion

You've made it to the end of this book, congratulations! It's my hope that this book lived up to the promise I made to you at the start. I want you to know that you can do this. That you feel that you can do this. That you see the path ahead of you and the impact your book is going to make on the lives of you and so many others.

Recap of Where You've Been

Chapter 1

We began with getting a solid understanding and a clear sense of the purpose, vision, and impact that you're looking to create in the lives of others. Revisit the workbook and see if how you started thinking about your book is the same as how you feel now.

Do you...

- Know your purpose?
- Have a clear vision?
- Know how you want your readers to be impacted?

Chapter 2

Your personal, professional, and business goals are a huge part of how you'll define success with your book. How are you feeling now? Have they changed at all?

Do you...

- Know your personal goals for your book?
- Know your professional goals for your book?
- Know your business goals for your book?

Chapter 3

We dove deep into how to get into the right mindset to ensure you have the right tools you'll need to make your book a reality. Do you have what you need to succeed?

Have you…

- Accepted that we all feel like imposters?
- Committed to yourself that you *will* finish writing this manuscript?
- Made peace with the fact that you'll need to take a mental health break or two during this process?

Chapter 4

Here we talked about accountability, structure, and having the right team. Are you feeling complete with the structures you currently have in place? Do you need more from somewhere?

Do you…

- Know who will play the role of Strategist, Therapist, and Cheerleader?
- Have your plan in place for when life will inevitably get in the way of your writing?
- Have a completion date set for when your manuscript will be written?

Chapter 5

This is when you really defined, in deep detail, who you're writing this book for. Has your target reader changed from when you started this book to now?

Do you…

- Have clarity on who exactly you're writing for?
- Understand what makes your target reader do what they do.
- Know where to find more information about your target reader?

Chapter 6

Here we discovered and discussed the ideal book length. Did you have a clear vision of your book's length before you began writing or planning it? Now that you have this information, has it changed since you started? Do you…

- Know how many words you want your manuscript to be?
- Know how many writing sessions it will take for you to complete your manuscript?
- Know when you want your draft manuscript written by?

Chapter 7

There are so many tools you can utilize to see success in getting your book written and published. How are you feeling about that? How are you planning on implementing the tips shared in this chapter?

Have you…

- Identified content that you can repurpose?
- Granted yourself permission to write a shitty first draft?
- Downloaded the worksheet to track your progress?

Chapter 8

Your first draft is inevitably going to be shitty, so we granted ourselves permission for it to be just that. Have you made peace with knowing that your first draft won't be perfect and it's an unrealistic goal to think it could be?

Have you…

- Created a mind map?
- Turned that mind map into a solid book outline?
- Decided the best writing program to write your manuscript in?

Chapter 9

Much of this book is about ease, efficiency, and strategy. There were many tips in this chapter to accomplish all three of these objectives. Are you comfortable with approaching the writing process differently than you have in the past?

Have you…

- Identified your writing routine?
- Used the Pomodoro technique?
- Created a parking lot of ideas that may not fit in your current book?

Chapter 10

The editing process is significant and often underrated. Are you feeling good about the editing plan you've laid out for yourself when you get to the point of needing an editor?

Do you…

- Understand the importance of self-editing?
- Know the differences between editing types?
- Have the guidance to push through when the editing process gets tough?

Chapter 11

Instead of jumping into publishing without any information, we talked about what your needs, wants, and desires are from the process. Are you feeling confident that your needs will be met when you hire a publisher?

Do you…

- Know what your needs, wants, and desires for your book are?
- Know what kind of relationship you're looking for with a publisher?
- Know your personal values and how they'll align with the publisher you choose?

CONCLUSION

Chapter 12

There are a lot of predatory companies in the publishing industry. Do you feel confident you'll know how to avoid them as you interview prospective publishers?

Do you...

- Have a general idea of the types of publishing paths available?
- Know whether you have more time versus money or vice versa in this process?
- Know how to spot a predatory publisher?

Chapter 13

Equally predatory behavior can be found through censoring your words as an author. Do you have a plan to ensure you're working with the right editor and/or publisher to avoid this?

Do you...

- Know how to protect your story in the publishing industry?
- Understand how editors may censor your words?
- Know how to select the right editor to work with?

Chapter 14

There are multiple publishing paths for you to pursue as an author. Do you have a sense of which publishing path feels best for you at this point in your journey?

Do you...

- Understand the top pros and cons of each publishing path?
- Understand the importance of having the right Publishing Strategist?
- Know what your assets are as an author?

Chapter 15

Understanding that you and your publisher are equal partners in the publishing of your book, you have every right to interview publishers and ask them a lot of questions. Do you know what you're going to ask during your next publisher call?

Do you...

- Know how to research prospective publishers?
- Know how to find out what kind of publisher they are?
- Know the right questions to ask to find an equitable publishing relationship?

Chapter 16

Publishing a book costs money regardless of what path you choose. Do you have a clearer understanding of where you'll need to make investments to get your book published and into the hands of your readers?

Do you...

- Have a better understanding of why you must invest in your book?
- Have a better understanding of how much it'll cost to publish your book?
- Understand how to get a return on your book investment?

Chapter 17

Having a strong sense of how long it takes to publish your book will provide you with proper expectations as you begin to follow the publishing path you've set for yourself.

Do you...

- Know how long it will take to publish your book?
- Understand the general publishing timeline based on what publishing path you choose?
- Know how to navigate the inevitable bumps in the road during the publishing process?

CONCLUSION

Chapter 18

Launching your book is a huge part of this process and requires celebration. But do you have a plan for what comes after your book is launched? Do you...

- Understand that you can't wait until your book is published to start marketing and promoting it?
- Have an idea of how you plan on launching your book when the time comes?
- Know what will come next after your book is published?

You've Got This!

If you've made it to the end of this book, I assure you that you're now in much better shape and have the skills and resources you need to get your book written and published. Often the biggest challenge in having written a manuscript is the sheer amount of overwhelm by what to do next once you have that first draft written. Now that you've made it through 67,080 words, it's my hope that you have the confidence you need to move forward in a way that feels right and authentic to you and your journey as an author. The following pages contain plentiful resources you can access anytime to get the support you need, wherever you might be in the process.

READER RESOURCES

If you just read the conclusion of this book and are still in the writing process, remember, just focus on getting your first draft completed. You can't do much else until that's done. A publisher can't publish words that you haven't written yet. But once you have that draft completed, the world will open up to you and your next steps will emerge.

Write at a pace that works for you. If you forget or have a moment of doubt, go back and reread Part 1 of this book. There's a delicate balance between meeting a goal you set and running yourself into the ground while doing so. You're on your own timeline, no one else's.

Writing Support

As you're finishing your manuscript, please take me up on the many free offers we've created at PYP. You've seen me mention in a number of places throughout this book that we have a number of free resources that can help you in the completion of your writing process.

30-Day Book Writing Challenge

When writing a book, it can be immeasurably helpful to have someone else impose some structure on your writing routine. If you sign up for our 30-Day Book Writing Challenge, you'll finally have a foolproof way to get your book written. In this challenge, join dozens of aspiring (or multi-book) authors who share a dream of getting their ideas down on paper and (finally!) getting that first draft over with.

You can find some of the tips, how to participate, and more information by going here: www.publishyourpurpose.com/30-day-book-writing-challenge.

Publish Your Purpose Author Lab

This is an online workshop that we, at PYP, run a couple of times a year. The goal is to really kickstart your writing process by providing you with a framework and foundation for discovering your purpose, your impact, and who you're writing for. Then, we dive into the details of how to actually get your writing done with a really specific formula to follow that will help make it happen. Essentially it's the first part of this book, but in video format.

You can find the replays from the last workshop I ran, a link to our private Facebook group, and a link to download the accompanying workbook by going to https://publishyourpurpose.com/author-lab/.

Getting Started for Authors

The Getting Started for Authors program is a six-month online course to get writers from the first word written on the page to finishing their manuscript (and being proud of it). We know exactly what you need to get there as a first-time author, and we've put it all together into one course. If you're looking for a real kick in the pants and support in getting your book written in six months, our Getting Started for Authors program may be exactly what you're looking for!

Accountability and Strategy Sessions

We know how hard it is to stick to writing deadlines, so we'll keep you accountable with one strategy session per week to make sure you're on track to hit your goals. This is a great time to seek strategic guidance from us when you're feeling stuck.

Writing Sessions

You'll meet with your writer's group once a week over Zoom for a designated time to write, so you don't miss your deadlines. With a personalized writing schedule, you'll begin to notice your writer's block melting away and becoming replaced by a consistent outpouring of content!

Peer Critiques

To finish your book, you need as many eyes on it as possible. Gain insight from your fellow writers. You'll have the opportunity to have your writing critiqued and reviewed by your peers in a safe and encouraging environment. Critiques are provided from a place of support and empowerment among the group, as we work to push each other to be better writers.

Organization Tools

Save precious time by using our tried-and-true methods of organization for your next book. This includes help with outlining, repurposing existing content from other things you've written, and working with an amazing software program called Scrivener that will absolutely change the way you think about your book. Plus we provide a progress tracker spreadsheet tool so you can visually see the progress you're making.

Writing Videos and Worksheets

Learn the best practices for improving your writing and producing a higher-quality book at the end of all your hard work. Our worksheets are tried and tested and have been used by me personally. Gain access to dozens of resources that are vetted and available to you as you continue to explore your publishing paths after your book is written (and we're always adding more). Learn more at https://publishyourpurpose.com/writing-support/.

If You're Ready To Publish

If you're ready to find a publisher, understand that everyone is on a journey of their own. What feels good for you won't for someone else, and vice versa. It's important to stay clear with your vision and not allow others to sway your vision so it accommodates an agenda they may be trying to push. You, as an author, have an equal stake in any publishing-related conversation—this is not a one-sided relationship. Be sure to properly advocate for yourself in this process!

Once your book is completed, many questions begin to arise about how to get your book published. We covered many of them in deep detail in Part 3 of this book; however, if you're looking for simpler guides that you can easily reference, you'll want to check out these free resources.

9 Questions to Ask a Publisher

In this guide, you'll find the top questions you should ask when reviewing any book publisher. It goes into detail on how to research prospective publishers, distinguish between the three main types of publishing houses, and gives you the nuanced questions to ask to ensure you're fully protected from predatory publishers. You can download it at www.publishyourpurpose.com/questions-ask-publisher.

Pick Your Path to Publishing Webinar

In this webinar, I break down the three available publishing paths to help you 1) identify the right path to publishing for you, 2) avoid predatory publishers, 3) evaluate the legitimacy of available service providers, and 4) publish a book that's aligned with your vision and values. You can watch it at www.publishyourpurpose.com/your-publishing-path-webinar.

Book Cost Blueprint

This blueprint breaks down the cost ranges by publishing type—and highlights factors to consider—so that you can make confident decisions about how to publish your book. You can download it at https://publishyourpurpose.com/book-cost-blueprint-optin/.

Publish Your Purpose

Additionally, if you'd like to see whether your manuscript is right for PYP, please get in touch with us by completing our Author Application form. From there, we'll schedule a time to meet with you to learn more about your vision and how we might be able to help you get there! Learn more at https://publishyourpurpose.com/publishing-support.

There's More Than Just Writing & Publishing

As you continue through the writing and publishing process, remember that all the times you're thinking about your book in the shower or giving a friend your book's elevator pitch over breakfast are examples of *you working on your book*. Don't judge your ability to get your book done just by the number of words on the page. All activities related to your book count.

Completing your book is crossing one finish line, and getting your book published is crossing a second finish line, but marketing your book is a finish line you never cross. It's a lifelong journey of making sure your prospective readers know about you and your book!

Join Our Community of Writers & Authors

I would love nothing more than to connect with you on social media. I'm at @jenntgrace everywhere, and Publish Your Purpose is @publishyourpurpose. I and the team are active on LinkedIn and in our Publish Your Purpose Author Lab Facebook group. I encourage you to join our Facebook group, introduce yourself, tell people what you're writing about, and witness the incredible generosity of other authors looking to give and receive support of their own.

As a result of reading this book (and maybe before), you now know that one of the biggest downsides of publishing a book is that as the author, you don't know who has read your book. You see the number of sales on a spreadsheet as a simple value. Unless you're super engaged as a reader, it's really hard to convince someone to leave the book and engage with you on social media or in some other type of fashion.

It's my hope that I've offered a lot of value to you throughout this book and that you see I genuinely care about the success of your book project. I also hope you'll connect with me on social media so that I can continue to champion you along the way. Jump on to social media and tag me. Tell me where you're at and what you need—I, and the PYP team, are here to support you! I want to see your success and toast you from afar as you cross those finish lines of writing and publishing!

GROW
FURTHER

To easily find all of the resources mentioned on the previous pages, visit the Publish Your Purpose Book Extras web page here:

https://publishyourpurpose.com/book-extras.

ABOUT JENN

An award-winning author, nationally recognized speaker, and savvy publishing strategist, Jenn T. Grace is the founder of Publish Your Purpose, the acclaimed hybrid publishing company that gives first-time authors the secrets to getting their books written, finding an eager audience, and marking their place in the publishing world. Publish Your Purpose is a certified B Corp social enterprise that meets the gold standard of socially and environmentally friendly business practices.

Jenn leads ambitious authors through every aspect of writing, editing, and publishing so that their books strategically align with their business objectives. Whether it's a business guide that shows the breadth of their expertise or an emotional memoir that takes readers deep into life's challenges, she helps authors articulate their purpose and fulfill their mission.

Jenn has published the books of almost 200 business owners, entrepreneurs, speakers, and memoirists so more diverse stories can exist in the world and her authors can make a positive impact and achieve the recognition and success they deserve. She's the author of seven books, including her memoir, *House on Fire*. Jenn has been featured in *Forbes*, *The Huffington Post*, *The Wall Street Journal*, and on CNBC.

Jenn lives in Connecticut with her family and enjoys being outside with her son, kayaking, hiking, skiing, and admiring the birds and nature around her.

You can follow Jenn on social media:
- www.Facebook.com/JennTGrace
- www.Instagram.com/JennTGrace
- www.LinkedIn.com/in/JennTGrace
- www.publishyourpurpose.com/podcast

HIRE JENN TO SPEAK

Make an impact at your next event with Jenn T. Grace as your keynote speaker.

Nationally recognized, she has spoken on a variety of topics including equitable publishing, LGBTQ+ inclusion in business and the workplace, leveraging the power of your personal brand by being uniquely you, and leading with empathy.

Jenn is a gifted storyteller and engages global audiences with her signature blend of honesty, humor, and savvy advice.

To learn more about how you can hire Jenn, please visit www.jenntgrace.com.

Ask Jenn about

- Publishing a non-fiction book or memoir
- Determining which publishing path is right for you
- Discovering why diversity in publishing/storytelling is important
- Learning about conscious capitalism and social entrepreneurship
- Starting and growing a business leveraging thought leadership as an author

ACKNOWLEDGMENTS

Writing a book is a labor of love that is not without a lot of ups and downs throughout the process. This book is a combination of over 10 years of experience in the publishing industry, which means the list of people to thank is extraordinarily long.

I often say that both writing and publishing are team sports—and I mean that. I'm fortunate to have an incredible team by my side at PYP.

In particular, I'd like to thank—

Niki Garcia, for being my constant sounding board since PYP was just an idea back in 2015. You are the glue that keeps this company efficiently running.

The editors and designers of this book. Without you, this book would not be what it is. A special thank you to Malka Wickramatilake, Nancy Graham-Tillman, Nelly Murariu, and Rebecca Pollock. You are truly the best team!

Our writers past and present. Throughout the years at PYP, we've had a number of incredible humans contribute content for our blog, our internal processes, and our marketing. These amazing people include Bailly Morse, Brandi Lai, Kendra Sand, Lily Capstick, Skye Miller, Stephanie Feger, Brandi Bernoskie, Taylor Beaven, and Elizabeth Oxendine. Throughout the creation of this book, I was able to go back in time and reference materials that you've helped cocreate, which gave me a great starting point to continue to teach our readers here.

All of my loved ones. I sincerely appreciate your patience with me as I've routinely ignored you in the evenings and weekends during the months of January and February of 2023, in a mad dash to meet my deadline of getting this manuscript complete. I love you—and thank you!

BIBLIOGRAPHY

Birnbaum, Debra. "'Homeland' Star Elizabeth Marvel: 'It's a Wonderful Time' to Be Playing the President-Elect." *Variety*. January 13, 2017. https://variety.com/2017/tv/news/homeland-star-elizabeth-marvel-its-a-wonderful-time-to-be-playing-the-president-elect-1201960319/.

Curcic, Dimitrije. "Bestselling Books Have Never Been Shorter [Study of 3,444 NYT Bestselling Titles]." WordsRated. June 20, 2022. https://wordsrated.com/bestselling-books-have-never-been-shorter/.

Donaldson, Emily. "What the Rise of the Memoir Has Meant for Non-Fiction." The Globe and Mail. September 17, 2021. https://www.theglobeandmail.com/arts/books/article-you-must-remember-this-the-rise-and-rise-of-memoir/.

Graesser A. C., M. Singer, and T. Trabasso. "Constructing Inferences During Narrative Text Comprehension." *Psychological Review* 101, no. 3 (1994): 371–395. https://doi.org/10.1037/0033-295x.101.3.371.

Heath, Chip, and Dan Heath. *Made to Stick: Why Some Ideas Survive and Others Die*. New York: Random House, 2007.

"Imposter Syndrome." *Psychology Today*. Accessed March 7, 2023. https://www.psychologytoday.com/us/basics/imposter-syndrome.

Klare, George R. *The Measurement of Readability*. Ames, IA: Iowa State University Press, 1963.

Ladouceur, Pat. "What We Fear More Than Death." MentalHelp.net. Accessed March 7, 2023. https://www.mentalhelp.net/blogs/what-we-fear-more-than-death/.

Milliot, Jim. "Self-Improvement Boom Sets Book Sales Off on Fast Start in 2021." Publishers Weekly. January 14, 2021. https://www.publishersweekly.com/pw/by-topic/industry-news/bookselling/article/85316-book-sales-get-off-to-fast-start.html.

Saad, Nardine. "Prince Harry's 'Spare' Ghostwriter Defends Book's Mistakes as It Breaks Sales Records." Los Angeles Times. January 12, 2023. https://www.latimes.com/entertainment-arts/books/story/2023-01-12/prince-harry-spare-errors-ghostwriter-sales.

Walsh, Neale Donald. *Conversations with God: An Uncommon Dialogue*. London, Hodder & Stoughton, 1997.

THE B CORP MOVEMENT

Dear Reader,

Thank you for reading this book and joining the Publish Your Purpose community! You are joining a special group of people who aim to make the world a better place.

What's Publish Your Purpose About?

Our mission is to elevate the voices often excluded from traditional publishing. We intentionally seek out authors and storytellers with diverse backgrounds, life experiences, and unique perspectives to publish books that will make an impact in the world.

Beyond our books, we are focused on tangible, action-based change. As a woman- and LGBTQ+-owned company, we are committed to reducing inequality, lowering levels of poverty, creating a healthier environment, building stronger communities, and creating high-quality jobs with dignity and purpose.

As a Certified B Corporation, we use business as a force for good. We join a community of mission-driven companies building a more equitable, inclusive, and sustainable global economy. B Corporations must meet high standards of transparency, social and environmental performance, and accountability as determined by the nonprofit B Lab. The certification process is rigorous and ongoing (with a recertification requirement every three years).

How Do We Do This?

We intentionally partner with socially and economically disadvantaged businesses that meet our sustainability goals. We embrace and encourage our authors and employee's differences in race, age, color, disability, ethnicity, family or marital status, gender identity or expression, language, national origin, physical and mental ability, political affiliation, religion, sexual orientation, socioeconomic status, veteran status, and other characteristics that make them unique.

Community is at the heart of everything we do—from our writing and publishing programs to contributing to social enterprise nonprofits, including reSET (www.resetco.org) and our work in founding B Local Connecticut (www.blocalct.com).

We are endlessly grateful to our authors, readers, and local community for being the driving force behind the equitable and sustainable world we're building together.

To connect with us online or publish with us, visit us at www.publishyourpurpose.com.

Elevating Your Voice,

Jenn T Grace

Jenn T. Grace
Founder, Publish Your Purpose